The North American Sketches

of

R. B. Cunninghame Graham

Robert Bontine Cunninghame Graham
'The Fencer'
by
Sir William Rothenstein
(*Dunedin Art Gallery, New Zealand*)

The

North American Sketches

of

R. B. Cunninghame Graham

Selected and edited with
Introduction, Notes, Glossary
and Bibliography

by

JOHN WALKER

EDINBURGH

SCOTTISH ACADEMIC PRESS

Published by
Scottish Academic Press Ltd.
33 Montgomery Street, Edinburgh EH7 5JX

Hardback ISBN 7073 0459 8
Limp ISBN 7073 0481 4

This book has been published with the help of a grant from the Canadian Federation for the Humanities, using funds provided by the Social Sciences and Humanities Research Council of Canada.

British Library Cataloguing in Publication Data
Cunninghame Graham, R. B.
    The North American sketches of R. B. Cunninghame Graham.
    I. Title   II. Walker, John, *1933-*
823'.8   PR4525.C2/

ISBN 0-7073-0459-8
ISBN 0-7073-0481-4 Pbk

6003626200

Printed in Great Britain by
Clark Constable, Edinburgh and London

To
my wife Irene

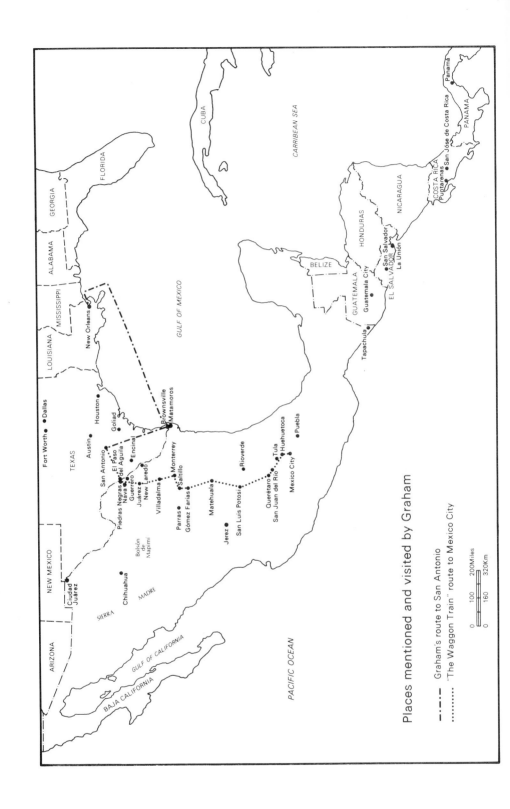

Places mentioned and visited by Graham

— · — · — Graham's route to San Antonio
· · · · · · · · · · "The Waggon Train" route to Mexico City

| 0 | 100 | 200 Miles |
| 0 | 160 | 320 km |

CONTENTS

Illustrations

Gabrielle Cunninghame Graham
by
G. P. Jacomb-Hood
(the hands, reputedly, by Whistler)
(*From a private collection*)

EDITOR'S FOREWORD

There is no doubt that there has been a revival of interest, if not exactly a boom, in the life and works of Robert Bontine Cunninghame Graham. Since I published *The South American Sketches of R. B. Cunninghame Graham* (Norman: University of Oklahoma Press, 1978), there have been two critical biographies, one in English and one in Spanish, superseding the two eulogistic biographies of the 1930s[1] — Alicia Jurado's *El escocés errante: R. B. Cunninghame Graham* (Buenos Aires: Emecé, 1978), which sits neatly alongside her biography of Graham's kindred spirit, W. H. Hudson, and the solid *Cunninghame Graham: A Critical Biography* (London: Cambridge University Press, 1979) by the long-time Graham scholars, Cedric Watts and Laurence Davies. Apart from my edition of *The Scottish Sketches of R. B. Cunninghame Graham* (Edinburgh: Scottish Academic Press, 1982), we have also seen the publication of *Beattock for Moffat and the Best of R. B. Cunninghame Graham* (Edinburgh: Paul Harris, 1979), and *Tales of Horsemen* (Edinburgh: Canongate, 1981). Though a small group of devotees, the Graham circle grows and is very active. One awaits with great anticipation the family-type biography by Graham's grand-niece, Lady Polwarth, now that the work of Alexander Maitland on Graham and his wife Gabrielle, which concentrates on marriage and politics, has recently appeared: *Robert and Gabriela Cunninghame Graham* (Edinburgh: Blackwood, 1984).

After many years of being treated as a fascinating character, protector and patron of other writers (Hudson, Conrad, Tschiffely, et al.), or at most an "amateur writer of genius," as some contemporaries labelled him, it looks as if Graham is finally coming into his own. Some thirty books, not to mention pamphlets, translations, prefaces, plus a voluminous correspondence,[2] represent a substantial output by a "part-time" writer. Unfortunately most of these books published between the 1890s and his death in 1936 are now out of print. The aim of this volume, as well as my past and future collections of Graham's work, is to make his writing available again, not only to scholars in the field, but also to the general public to whom he dedicated so many ingeniously titled prefaces over the years.

I am grateful to the late Admiral Sir Angus Cunninghame Graham (deceased 1981) and Lady Cunninghame Graham for their unfailing help, hospitality and co-operation since the early 1960s; also to their daughter Lady Polwarth for her unflagging support and spirited encouragement, and for her permission to consult, copy and reproduce many of the family letters, papers and documents, originally in the family home at Ardoch and now at the Harden home of Lord and Lady Polwarth, and also to reproduce the sketches contained in this volume. I am grateful also to the staff at various libraries for their help and collaboration during this research and other Graham work: the National Library of Scotland, Edinburgh; the Mitchell Library, Glasgow; Baillie's Library, Glasgow; the Baker Library, Dartmouth College, Hanover, New Hampshire; Humanities Research Centre, University of Texas at Austin; Douglas Library, Queen's University, Kingston, Ontario. I should like to express my thanks also to the School of Graduate Studies and Research, Queen's University, for the valuable travel and research grants which have facilitated the investigation and the publication of this and other material on Cunninghame Graham over the years; to my daughter Clare for typing this manuscript, my wife Irene for her patient and careful proof-reading, and Eleanor Smith for valuable secretarial assistance; to my colleagues Ross Hough and Dr George Lovell for the production of the map; to Lady Cunninghame Graham for her permission to use the reproduction of the Jacomb-Hood portrait of Gabriela; to Lady Polwarth and the Dunedin Art Gallery, New Zealand for permission to use the reproduction of the Rothenstein portrait of Robert, "The Fencer".

NOTES

1. H. F. West. *A Modern Conquistador: Robert Bontine Cunninghame Graham: His Life and Works* (London: Cranley and Day, 1932); and A. F. Tschiffely. *Don Roberto: Being the Account of the Life and Works of R. B. Cunninghame Graham 1852-1936* (London: Heinemann, 1937).

2. Most of it is still uncollected, and can be found at various places, especially at Harden, Hawick, Scotland, the family estate of Lord and Lady Polwarth; the National Library of Scotland, Edinburgh; the Baker Library, Dartmouth College, Hanover, New Hampshire; the Humanities Research Centre, University of Texas at Austin. See also in collected form *W. H. Hudson's Letters to R. B. Cunninghame Graham*, edited by Richard Curle (London: Golden Cockerel Press, 1941); and *Joseph Conrad's Letters to R. B. Cunninghame Graham*, edited by Cedric T. Watts (London: Cambridge University Press, 1969).

INTRODUCTION

by

JOHN WALKER

In the Editor's Foreword to my edition of *The South American Sketches of R. B. Cunninghame Graham* (1978) I promised that other collections would follow, in an attempt to make Graham's writings available again to the wider reading public. Since that date my volume of *The Scottish Sketches of R. B. Cunninghame Graham* has already appeared (1982), and I am now at work on Graham's Spanish sketches, with the North African pieces to follow.

Born in London, Graham travelled extensively in Spain and South America, and was finely tuned to the life and customs of these regions. As a companion volume to *The South American Sketches*, I now present *The North American Sketches*, embracing his life and writings as they apply to Mexico, Texas and South-West U.S.A. This part of his life is perhaps less well known — hence the doubts and shadowy, even erroneous, facts that have emerged about his stay there, as treated in the early biographies of West and Tschiffely. The number of sketches about this region is much smaller than his group of River Plate sketches, for example. This should not surprise us, since he spent only two years in North America, and thus had less material with which to work. One, therefore, should have certain reservations about the theory of one critic who attributes the paucity of Graham's writings on this region to the sense of failure that he experienced in his material and commercial dealings; and thus chose not to write about them.[1]

Graham has given the lie to this theory with the production of some of his best sketches that grew out of this visit, like "Un Pelado" and "A Hegira," which constitute an important part of his life and his literary career. One must remember that he went immediately to North America after his marriage and spent the first two years of his married life there. In literary, political, historical and cultural terms, he retained a great interest in this region for the rest of his life. His correspondence contains many letters from Frederick R. Guernsey, an American journalist in Mexico City, who was to be his contact in Mexico for many years long after Graham's return to Britain.[2] Even at home he devoted letters to the press on Mexico and South-West U.S.A., and book reviews in publications like the *English Review*, *The Nation* and the *Saturday Review*, as late as 1935, the year before his death.[3] The fact that the stories, sketches and letters which comprise this volume span a period of four decades from the 1890s till the mid-1930s indicates his long-standing interest in, and feeling for, Mexico, Texas and South-West U.S.A.

Life and Works: A Summary

Although Graham was only in his late twenties when he set off for Texas in 1879, he had already had enough adventure to satisfy most men for the rest of their lives. But Graham was by temperament, family background and upbringing attracted to the New World. His mother was born in 1828 on the British flagship H.M.S. *Barham* between Jamaica and Venezuela. Her father, Admiral Elphinstone Fleeming, who had married Catalina Paulina Alesandro from Cádiz, had been making the British presence felt in the Caribbean during the Spanish-American Wars of Independence of the first decades of the nineteenth century, and had gained some fame for his dealings with Simón Bolívar, the Great Liberator, and José Antonio Páez, the hero of Venezuelan independence.

Robert, although born in 1852 in London, where his father Major Bontine was garrisoned with the Scots Greys, spent most of his youth at Finlaystone and Gartmore, the family estates in Scotland. Before he went off to school in England, he had already acquired a passion for horses and riding that was to stay with him for the rest of his life, and was to be of great use to him in his future adventures in North and South America. His education at Harrow and later in Brussels was to provide him with a knowledge of fencing and languages, to add to the horse-riding and Spanish which he absorbed through his family connections.

In 1870, when he finished his formal education, young Robert decided to seek adventure and fortune, and, not surprisingly, given his background, plus his knowledge of Spanish and horses, he chose the New World, in particular the pampas of Argentina. Embroiled in revolutions in Argentina and commercial enterprises in Paraguay, Roberto was to stay there till 1873. Home again, he befriended George Mansel, the son of a Dorset landowner, with whom he set sail again for Argentina where they were soon involved in horse-dealing between Uruguay and Brazil.

Back in Europe in 1878, he met the mysterious Gabrielle de la Balmondière, as she was known, and married her against the wishes of his family. After a year trying to put the family estate at Gartmore in order, the young couple decided to set off for Texas, where during that era of nineteenth-century progress, fortunes were to be made in the cattle business — at least, that is what the advertising brochures claimed. After two years of various enterprises, commercial, fencing, ranching and other cattle activities (for Robert), and painting and teaching (for Gabriela), they returned to Europe in 1881, and to Britain in 1883 on the death of his father. Robert Bontine Cunninghame Graham, as he was now called, took over the family estates at Gartmore and Ardoch — debts and all.

By 1886 the radical spirit, which he had acquired on the pampas and plains of North and South America in the face of injustice, cruelty and tyranny, nurtured for a decade through observation of inequalities at home and meetings with socialists like Keir Hardie, brought about his election to Parliament as Liberal member for North-West Lanark. For six years Graham was to achieve fame and notoriety for progressive ideas and fiery speeches on behalf of the exploited working-classes. Nor was he averse to resorting to vigorous action to uphold his principles. On 13 November 1887 he took part in the infamous "Bloody Sunday" demonstration in Trafalgar Square on behalf of the imprisoned Irish M.P. William O'Brien and the principle of free speech. For his efforts he received brutal treatment from the police, was arrested, and sent to Pentonville gaol for six weeks.

When he lost his seat in Parliament in 1892, the eccentric in him took him on a fruitless gold hunt to Spain, based on Pliny's description of ancient Lusitania.[4] Then in 1897 he tried to reach Tarudant, the Forbidden City in Morocco, which had never been entered by a Christian. Though unsuccessful in both enterprises, he had acquired the material for future literary efforts. The North African adventure was retold in *Mogreb-el-Acksa* (1898), one of the most exciting travel books ever written, and the source of George Bernard Shaw's *Captain Brassbound's Conversion*.

With the end of his official political duties and his exotic travel adventures, Robert embarked on a literary career that was to continue till his death forty years later, during which period he produced almost a book a year. They were mostly collections of stories based on his early experiences in North and South America, North Africa, Europe, and of course Britain, especially Scotland, plus histories, biographies, and travel books.

As early as 1895 he had already produced *Notes on the District of Menteith*, about the region he knew so well, around the family home at Gartmore. *Father Archangel of Scotland* (1896) was a collection of essays and sketches produced in collaboration with his wife. The pieces of *The Ipané* (1899), *Thirteen Stories* (1900), *Success* (1902), *Progress* (1905), *His People* (1906), as well as his Latin American histories, *A Vanished Arcadia* (1901) and *Hernando de Soto* (1903), were all published before the tragic death of his wife in 1906. Despite his grief, already great with the earlier loss of the family home at Gartmore in 1901, after a period of mourning and inactivity Graham managed to produce from his other estate at Ardoch and in London, with his mother's encouragement, further collections of his unique sketches — *Faith* (1909), *Hope* (1910), *Charity* (1912), and *A Hatchment* (1913). With the outbreak of war in 1914, Graham, at the age of sixty-two, offered his services as a Rough Rider, belying the notion that he was anti-patriotic because of his earlier scathing attacks on British imperial and colonial policy in Africa, Asia and elsewhere.[5] Though too old for active service, he was appointed honorary colonel and dispatched to the scene of his youth, South America, to buy horses for the army. Meanwhile, his history of colonial Latin America, *Bernal Díaz del Castillo* (1915), and his collection of stories, *Brought Forward* (1916), were published while he was on government business.

After the war he took up the pen again to continue his series of histories of

the colonial, independence and post-independence periods of Latin America —
A Brazilian Mystic (1920), *Cartagena and the Banks of the Sinú* (1922), *The Conquest of New Granada* (1922), *The Conquest of the River Plate* (1924), *Pedro de Valdivia* (1926), *José Antonio Páez* (1929), and *The Horses of the Conquest* (1930). As the war trips had been the source of the Brazilian, Argentine and Colombian histories, so too were the Venezuelan histories a result of a sentimental journey that he had made in 1925 to the scene of his mother's birth, prompted by her death in the same year at the age of ninety-seven.

In the last decade of his life when he was not travelling abroad to places like Ceylon and South Africa to spare his weakening health the rigours of a British winter, he spent time writing at the family home at Ardoch and in London. Sandwiched between his Latin American histories was the biography of his famous ancestor, Robert Graham of poetic renown, *Doughty Deeds* (1925). During his last years also he formed a sentimental attachment with the Scottish National Party, on whose behalf he spoke vigorously at meetings throughout the country. Although always the Scotsman, Graham was too much of a cosmopolitan figure to be restricted by the parochial limitations of a narrow nationalism.

After his various trips abroad and the publication of his last works, *Portrait of a Dictator* (1933), an ominous indictment of Solano López and *his* special form of tyranny at a time of growing Fascism in Europe, and his final collection of sketches, *Writ in Sand* (1932) and *Mirages* (1936), he decided at the age of eighty-three to make the final pilgrimage to his first love, Argentina, which he wanted to visit one more time before his imminent death. Not surprisingly, given his health and the arduous journey, he died in Buenos Aires on 20 March 1936.

Having been honoured by the Argentines, from gaucho to President of the Republic, his body was brought home to Scotland to be buried beside his wife in the ruined Augustinian priory on the island of Inchmahome, situated on the Lake of Menteith, where he was welcomed and mourned by his own people. The following year 1937 a monument was erected at Castlehill, Dumbarton, near the family home at Ardoch, where it stood for over forty years, resisting the ravages of time, weather and vandalism. Only recently (1981) was it removed and re-erected close to the original family estate at Gartmore. As his epitaph states, he truly was "A Master of Life. A King Among Men."

Cunninghame Graham in Mexico, Texas and South-West U.S.A.

Of Graham it was once said that there was no need to write his biography, since his life was contained in his writings. Of course, there is much of the man in his works, and that is one of the attractions of the sketches. But there is still a great deal of mystery about several aspects of his life, the investigation of which I leave to those who feel qualified to comment, and to the literary detectives and sceptics who will surely invent what they cannot find.

His wife Gabrielle is undoubtedly an enigma, and their life together in the

New World just after their marriage, which constitutes the basis of this collection, is one of the shadowy periods about which there has been a great deal of speculation and difference of opinion amongst scholars. H. F. West is not very helpful in his 1932 biography, although he does quote an interesting letter to him by Don Roberto (written in 1931, fifty years after the event!) about the waggon train to Mexico.[6] A. F. Tschiffely has much more material, having had access to many (if not all) of the Graham papers for his 1937 biography. However, his account is also unreliable for several reasons. Like West, he wrote very much under the influence of the master, as a hero-worshipper, and thus perpetuated the mythology, if not the mythification, of Cunninghame Graham — which Graham himself, who was not averse to elaborating a little as the events receded into the dim regions of his memory, may have contributed to in his many conversations with Tschiffely. Whatever the motives, Tschiffely's rendering of the Texas episode is unreliable, especially in the chronology, since he has Graham still in Texas in 1883. Fortunately much of the original Graham correspondence is still preserved, and one can fill in many gaps from his letters, although, apart from the obvious difficulties in trying to decipher his barbarous handwriting, Graham has the infuriating habit of omitting the year.[7] Thus, because of some garbled, mangled, and even erroneous transcriptions and interpretations, not to mention arbitrary omissions, the Tschiffely version is not totally credible, although his motives were always of the best.

Fortunately Tschiffely's biography has been superseded recently by the solid *Cunninghame Graham: A Critical Biography* of Cedric Watts and Laurence Davies, who have been much more scholarly, careful and assiduous in their investigation and documentation. However, the dearth of material on the Grahams' stay in North America, combined with Graham's surprising silence in his letters home as to his activities in Texas and the South-West, has reduced this episode to a mere six pages even in this admirable biography. Despite the paucity of details in the correspondence, the letters to his mother (and occasionally to friends) are still the main source of information on the North American stay, and I have used these as my principal fount of knowledge for this period of Graham's life.

I have been greatly helped in my efforts to pin down the events of this period by Lady Polwarth who has also confirmed many of my conclusions. Her own future biography of Don Roberto should be an absolute mine of information about many aspects of Graham's personal and family life hitherto not revealed. My own energies in this volume have been directed mainly to setting the facts straight, mostly with a view to making the sketches more meaningful and entertaining to the reader, and trying to link the sketches with Graham's experiences in this region. This approach should in no way be taken as an invitation to view the sketches solely as documents or sources of information. I have long advocated that we should read Graham's stories as works of art, as manifestations of his literary skill, not just as pamphlets, source books, and history or geography texts.[8] A reading of the correspondence, which

I have tried to fuse into the narrative of the events in Texas and the South-West, in order to make the Grahams' life more intelligible to the reader, will be complemented by the reading of the stories that follow, since the letters illumine the sketches and vice-versa.

Although the Mexico, South-West U.S.A. episode was rather a brief one in Graham's very full life, as we have noted, it was important not only as the initial period in his marriage, but also because it provided him with material that he was to use in later life, for his interesting sketches on this region.

After his exciting adventures in Argentina, Uruguay, Paraguay and Brazil in the 1870s, young Robert was restless on his return to Britain, and decided to travel to Europe in 1878. In Paris he met Gabrielle de la Balmondière, a young convent-educated French-Chilean orphan of obscure background, as most modern Graham scholars are quick to agree. Despite the opposition of his mother, Robert whisked Gabriela off to London where they were married on 24 October 1878 in a registry-office ceremony that did not please his family. The cold relations between Gabriela and her mother-in-law, Mrs. Bontine, were to persist, and are evident in the correspondence of both. Though the marriage of Robert and Gabriela was not a conventional marriage in the sense that they often went their separate ways, they did work together for a year to try and put Gartmore in some kind of order before departing in 1879 for Texas, to try and make their fortune.

In April 1879 they sailed for New Orleans, with the final intention of breeding cattle in or near Brownsville, across the Río Grande from Matamoros. Graham's informative observations on the people, the customs, the animals, and the places that he visited are worth recording. Here are his first impressions of New Orleans in a letter to his mother dated 18 May [1879]:[9]

> I arrived yesterday. We had a splendid passage, not a rough day all the way. It is very hot. New Orleans is lovely, quite flat, but the trees are splendid. All it needs is a few white Spanish houses, as the wooden houses are all very well but as soon as a rich citizen builds a mansion the old Anglo Saxon vulgarity steps in & Ionic columns with Doric capitals, the whole finished with a Gothic (strangulated) spire is the order of the day. This is a completely ruined place. Before the war it was the rival of New York & had almost six hundred thousand inhabitants. Now there are only one hundred and eighty thousand. The town covers an immense extent of ground, & the magnolias, oleanders etc. are splendid.
>
> I think that here one realizes the south more than anywhere (I mean as in opposition to the Northern States). Long lank faces abound, feet are elevated (on chairs) high above the head, & everyone chews. To speak to they are decidedly better than the Northern people. There is no enormous quantity of "Nigs" to be seen in the streets. Quite as much French as English seems to be spoken. . .

The Brownsville boat, Sir, sails on Thursday, Sir, and takes about three days. Hence I think my next move will be to Hidalgo about eighty miles off. Pingo[10] is not very good here, but the mules are very fine. I should like old pingo out here as it is too hot to walk. I saw a Chinaman & two Indians this morning. . . The British Sabbath reigns here with all its accustomed horror and want of charity. When I add that the principal church (I have not seen the Roman Catholic cathedral yet) has a yellow pine gothic door with sham iron clasps on it, I think that you will understand the sham respectability of the city. . .

There is no doubt that these remarks are as much revealing of Graham himself as they are of New Orleans in 1879. His comments on the respectability and vulgarity of Anglo-Saxon civilisation and other manifestations of progress prefigure some of his best and most biting attacks on the triple-headed monster Civilisation/Progress/Commerce that one finds in sketches written some thirty years later, as in "Niggers" and "Success," for example. His own reference to "Nigs" should be taken more as a colloquialism rather than a display of racism, a sin of which he was never guilty. In fact, his whole literary output is a defence of the savage, barbarous races (in Africa and America) against the nefarious designs and exploitation by all the imperialist powers, not only Britain.

Within two weeks he was in Brownsville, writing to Mrs. Bontine, and complaining about the dreadful boat journey from New Orleans. In a letter dated 2 June [1897] he goes on:

... Pingo is here in large quantities. I have a black one that cost £4. He is pretty good but rather out of condition. The Mexican saddle is very picturesque but not the least like the recado. Pingo is very cheap here, indeed almost cheaper than in the River Plate.

The people are a little like the gauchos, but do not wear long hair like them, or dress in any particular kind of costume. The only curious thing they wear is a hat with a large band of silver and silver flowers embroidered on it. . .

I am trying to get a small place for breeding mules, from a man called Casimiro Tamayo, a curious old chap, speaking just like a gaucho. . . Matamoros, a large Mexican town of about 15,000 (souls), is about a mile from here, on the other side of the Rio Grande. It is very picturesque, the plaza and streets quite Spanish, the same aimless officers wandering listlessly about with a burnt out cigarette in their mouths & wondering whether either the government will ever pay their arrears (due 18 months) or if they will meet a friend with a match about him; in either case they are quite resigned; in the one case to steal the first box of matches they can find, or to rob the first person handy of a dollar for God's sake.

Hence it is like getting into another world from Brownsville; the people all riding about on good horses and silver mounted saddles, while here the hair rope or old moke is all they afford. It is however far too dangerous on the other side of the Rio Grande to think of living there...

For this reason, and out of deference to his wife's safety,[11] Graham decided to move from the border town which, like others of its kind, attracted the worst elements from both sides of the Río Grande. Graham, who survived more violent brushes with the Argentine gaucho bandits in the 1870s, was perfectly capable of looking after himself, and did so on at least one occasion, if we are to believe Tschiffely's enigmatic reference to a "serious incident with a certain gentleman who came out second best" (Tschiffely, p. 143).

Within another couple of weeks he had decided to settle further up the coast in Corpus Christi. Two letters to his mother and a Mr. Wright, both dated 17 June, confirm his opinion that Brownsville was "too uncivilised a place to live in," and "too dangerous a place for settling in." Graham's letters of this period give fascinating accounts not only of *his* existence, but of the whole way of life of a people at this changing time in American history. The fact that he is British, therefore detached and objective, gives a special value to his comments and observations, reminiscent of the contribution of the British travellers to Argentine history in the nineteenth century. The letter to his mother, as always, is particularly informative in its description of Corpus Christi, and like all his correspondence provides a fascinating commentary to his travels:

Here it is on the sea, and the people are almost all Mexicans too, but quieter than the frontier. I think there is a street here that would lay over anything in "Red Dog". The place is very like one of Bret Harte's places, the same loafers, pingos, Mexicans etc & the same intermixture of Germans and French.

If this is Cuerpo de Cristo, donde está enterrada el alma del licenciado?[12] Pingo came up the hundred & sixty miles of almost desert country very well indeed, and he is now eating outside the window. Jack (the dog) came about 50 leagues & then had to be brought on in the stage coach.

Texas is not nearly so nice as the River Plate but some of the old Mexicans are very like the gauchos...

We stopped one day in the heat at a Mexican's house who had no horses and only four tame bulls. He said, "esos son todo mi capital, y a este torito quiero como a una hija."[13] Most of the land about here belongs to two men, King and Kennedy (of Cathlis [?] & of Kennedy), both of whom came here without a cent, & who I believe are unmitigated rascals both of them, but of course "a mask of gold hides all the deformities." Or perhaps as it is Texas we live in a lasso of gold... Ponchos are not worn here, but curiously enough the hat many of the Mexicans wear is the same as the picadores use in the bullfight.

> There are a good many nigs here as they many of them congregated after the war. I have got a nig servant & have taken a nice little house planted round with tamarisks and oleanders, while I am looking for a suitable location here. . . There are about ten different "choches" here all hating one another for the love of God in the usual style. . .

Despite his initial optimism, however, within a month he was bitterly disillusioned, not only with the weather and the land, but also with the horses, and especially with the people. On 25 July 1879 he was writing to his mother from Corpus Christi:

> Ye old weather is still going on. Here it is awfully hot and there has been no rain for eight months. . .

> Words are inadequate for the citizens about here, their meanness, hypocrisy and assassination, being beyond bounds. I don't believe in Italy in the Middle Ages there was so much assassination as there is in Texas today. Every day there is one or two. Such a thing as a fair fight is unknown, and if you enquire how so 'n so was killed, "I guess Sir — waited for him in the Chaparral & shot him in the back Sir". The Baptist is the most prevalent form of Christianity.

> Two Texans called respectively "Broncho Bill" and Sam (cognomen unknown) (Broncho is only an aguomen) meeting on opposite sides of the River & being unable to shake hands, Broncho remarks. Say Sam, it's a pity we can't shake hands. Let's go down stream a bit & have a friendly shot at one another. At the first fire, Sam called out "hello ol' man you've broke the pummel of my saddle; darn it remarked Broncho you went better than that, you got about two inches into my left arm; well old fellow goodbye, tell the folks to [at?] home I met you, & we had a good time together." Mind & tell cousin John this episode of life in a country untrammeled by an effete code of laws.

Despite his great sense of humour, Graham had had enough of Corpus Christi, and by 3 August he was writing to his mother to inform her that he was moving to San Antonio, levelling the same criticism against Corpus Christi that had prompted his move from Brownsville — "not very healthy and rather dangerous to live in."[14]

> . . . The country is very ugly all covered with dense low scrub and not such a thing as an open pampa. The people of all the people I ever came across are revolting and mean to a degree. The Mexicans are the only redeeming feature & they are not strictly speaking agreeable as they are chiefly thieves and murderers exiled from Mexico.

However, they are civil to speak to. The pitiful wooden houses are most repulsive, & I long to see one of the white Spanish houses of the River Plate. They say San Antonio is the most endurable place in Texas. The ruins of the old Missions are there. I wish I had gone down to Mexico instead of coming into Texas from Brownsville. My old pingo is getting very fat. Pingo is cheap here, as cheap as in the River Plate but on the average a little smaller and not so stoutly built. Corpus is not adapted for shipping lines as the harbour only admits small schooners. In fact all down the coast the harbours are bad and the Norther very violent one time of year, so that unless shipping lines were started except on very favourable terms I don't think it would succeed. . . It is still very hot here and there is a great want of water. . . There is a lot of people near here who have got religion (methodist form), and really seem as if they worshipped God for spite.

Not surprisingly, Graham did not delay, leaving this unpleasant place for San Antonio (de Bexar, as it was called then), where he arrived on 25 August after a seventeen-day journey to cover the one hundred and fifty miles from Corpus Christi. Bogged down by luggage and muddy roads, they had stopped for several days at an Irish settlement, whose inhabitants were "as dirty, evil and lying as Irishmen in other parts of the world." His first letter to his mother two days after his arrival, dated 27 August [1879], gives a good contemporary picture of that city:

San Antonio is by far the most picturesque place in Texas, & in the time of the Mexicans must have been wonderfully so. It is intersected in all directions by the river, & by little irrigation canals like in Spain. The place was made by the Duke of Bexar who was governor here, and imported a great many families from the Canary Islands. The old missions are all in ruins but I have not had time to go & see them yet. The churches in the town are mostly in ruins, but one next to this street (calle de las Salinas). There is an old Spanish church being restored & a stone tablet sets forth it to be the first Presbyterian church. The cross has been taken down & an effigy of the Rev. Samuel B. Edwards has been placed in its stead. The pulpit according to universal Presbyterian use has been placed in the chancel, & is about twenty feet high with sounding board and red velvet (cotton) cushions, & long tassels hanging also according to primitive use. Though the church is large & the worshippers but few, (all their friends & relations having been confined to the pit), a gallery is in contemplation. . . No one in Texas stirs without his rifle. Our guide this time was not a fat old Mexican like the one that came from Brownsville, but a dirty disagreeable American. . . I saw a Mexican Methodist preacher the other day. He was on pingo of course, black

clothes, white tie, Mexican hat, & a bulge at his back indicated that
he had either a bible or pistol there.

By the end of September Graham seemed reasonably settled in San
Antonio, looking around for business prospects, though it could not compare
with Argentina. In a letter to his mother dated 16 September he confesses: "I
am getting a little more reconciled to the "estado de Tejas" but it is not the
Pampa. What I miss most is the boundless view and the "gaucho" who does not
exist here. The Mexican is a splendid horseman very picturesque, but he is a
peasant & is not wild looking como el gaucho del Plata, but he is fun before el
gauchero . . ."

Though Graham was adamantly opposed to racial prejudice and bigotry,
he himself had made a few value judgments about the qualities of the various
races in the Wild West: "Servants are the most intolerable nuisance here. The
'nigs' are so fanciful they hardly ever stay more than a week. They are also
awfully insolent. The Mexicans are civil but steal everything, & no white
people, that is dirty Irish and German girls ever live out in Texas. They all get
married as soon as they arrive. . ." At least Graham had the decency to put in
quotation marks "nigs," indicating that this was the accepted designation of the
time and place, and not his.

By 1 October (in a letter to his mother) he is still complaining of the
weather and the country, which he seems to be getting used to, though he finds
the heat unbearable and the low bush country very ugly. Despite his comments
on the Indians and the Mexicans, in whom he saw no Rousseauesque vision of
the noble savage, his stay in Texas helped him to articulate his views on the
exploitation of the native peoples by the colonial powers, whether it be the
British in various parts of the empire, or the Americans with their then growing
views on manifest destiny, dollar diplomacy and the policy of the big stick.
Although he had no illusions about the Mexicans and the Indians, as his letters
demonstrate and as the sketches will confirm, the longer he lived in North
America the more he came to resent their ill-treatment. If his radical ideas had
been born on the pampas of Argentina, they were honed and sharpened in the
South-West, preparing the way for his future defence of Scottish miners,
English nail-makers, Zulu warriors and other oppressed minorities whom he
defended before, during and after his official political career. In one letter from
San Antonio (to his mother) dated 1 November 1879 in which he praises the
Indians' sartorial taste and equestrian skill, but not their treacherous character,
he ends with an emotional outburst against the barbaric conduct of the so-
called civilised nations:

The American mob and press is even more indecently elated with an
Indian victory than the English, if a rare occasion [?], as in the case of
Major Tharburgh's [?] affair with the Utes. Notices appear in the
newspapers in large type. Horrible massacre of white men. Death.
Blood. Scalps. The Indian again. Citizens to the front. Glory to God.

Hallelujah. Why is it both in England & America, when white troops win it is victory & when beaten, is it termed a horrible massacre. I always thought massacre meant when the murdered could not resist.

The tone of this letter shows a marked difference to his earlier ones, and anticipates the virulent letters of 1890 on the Indian Question which he sent to the *Daily Graphic*.

Still searching for commercial success after a few months in San Antonio, Robert and Gabrielle set out for Mexico City with a waggon-train of cotton. In his youth Graham always had profit-making schemes, whether it be selling cattle in Brazil, or obtaining maté concessions in Paraguay — all without success, of course. There seems to have been some doubt as to whether Graham was actually selling the cotton or simply travelling with the waggon-train. However, despite many of the Tschiffely myths, it would appear, according to Graham's letter of 19 January [1880], that he was in fact trying to sell the cotton. The waggon-train journey is a fact, and the dangerous adventures that he and his wife experienced are recorded and immortalised in her meticulously detailed, if not very artistic, sketch entitled simply "The Waggon-Train," included in this volume. Thus one need not repeat her description of this ordeal that lasted almost two months and was fraught with incident and danger.

By 19 January 1880 they had crossed the Río Grande and were well into Mexico. Writing from Monterrey, Robert informs his mother of the difficulty of the journey and the hostility of the cold weather. It is interesting to compare this letter with Gabriela's sketch which covers some of the same material. Robert was certainly not initially disappointed with Monterrey, which was the first "responsible" place they had seen since leaving San Antonio:

This is a wonderfully picturesque place, much more Spanish than the River Plate towns. The town is quite shut in by a spine of the Rocky Mountains & has a very pretty little river flowing through it. I started from San Antonio with a train of cotton waggons but had a dispute with the man & got out at a place called D'Hansus [?] in Texas and had to wait a week in the most awful cold I ever experienced. From there I went on to the frontier, & had to wait a fortnight to get on & finally came with the captain who was coming here to pay the frontier troops. All the way there was novedad of Los Indios which culminated one day in a place called El Tarumán by our finding an Indian arrow on the road, & meeting two men who had seen some horsemen galloping among the rocks & supposed they were Comanches or Lipanes. However, nothing happened, though five days before they killed a whole family leaving only a little child that hid itself in some bushes.

Graham himself was not immune to the dangers of the trail, and in fact even seemed to attract them, as he had done as a young man in Argentina in the previous decade. On discovering that the captain was plotting to kill them and take their horses and their arms, Robert decided that they should stay there and await a stray party with whom they should make the final twenty days journey to Mexico City. In the meanwhile he carried a revolver, a Winchester, a sword, and a knife — and even armed thus he did not feel safe!

Whilst resting, and glad to be out of Texas, Graham is his usual observant self. Here he makes one of his several references to his fascination with the Kickapoos whom he found in this region: "Here in Monterrey the remnant of the Kickapoos are living. They fought their way from up in the States down to here, & have been at war with the States for the last 150 years. They walk about the streets here in moccasins & always carry a rifle when in the town. There are nearly about a hundred of them left here but there are some more of them in a place called Santa Rosa. . ."

After a delay of several weeks, the travellers were ready to proceed, having become bored with Monterrey, which they found dull, though pretty and quaint. In a letter to his mother dated 6 February 1880[15] he announces his travel plans which involve going first to San Luis Potosí: "The road is all through mountains and is said to be very pretty, but not so safe as travelling in Texas on account of the thieves. But there are no Indians. . ." — only the favoured Kickapoos, who are described as "tall, thin with long hair & a much finer type than the low class Mexicans who are of the Aztec type short & stout & flat nosed. . ." — not to mention sullen and treacherous, though they do have the saving grace of taking good care of the horses.

The rest of the journey from San Luis Potosí to Mexico City via Querétaro, as described by Gabrielle in "The Waggon-Train," was hardly the *grand tour* prescribed for elegant young ladies of the nineteenth century — Indian raids, howling coyotes, bloody murders, Mescalero prisoners, Mexican brutality, marauding bandits, dust-covered roads, scorched plains, cactus, blind beggars and water-sellers. Many years later in a letter to H. F. West, dated 24 July 1931, Graham described, in complementary fashion to his wife's sketch, some of their adventures thus:

> On the journey from San Antonio to Mexico City I went with a wagon train carrying cotton as far as San Luis Potosi. I rode a black Mexican horse that I bought on the Rio Grande not far from Brownsville, Texas. My wife had a little grey Mustang mare, one of the tamest and at the same time most excitable horse I have ever ridden. She died upon the road upon Monterrey and Saltillo. During the journey we had a brush with the Lipan Apaches, but beat them off, after forming the wagons into a corral, just as you may see in the film The Covered Wagon. We had built a screen of brushwood round the wagons, not continuous but in the form of isolated shelters, possibly about 6 feet high.
>
> During the night my little fox terrier Jack kept on barking.

Taking off most of my clothes, after a good roll in the sand I crawled out to one of the shelters carrying my Winchester. It was very dark and after remaining four or five minutes at the shelter and seeing nothing I crawled back again. At day light feeling somehow that there had been someone on the other side of the bushes I went and looked and found the marks of an Indian's feet and knees where he had been kneeling, no doubt with his bow ready, not 12 feet from where I stood holding my rifle. Luckily for both of us, or perhaps one of us, neither could see the other in the darkness. Where he rides now, or if he rides, for in all probability his bones have mouldered long ago in the hot sands of Arizona, I do not know; but as I sit dictating this the whole scene comes back to me including the trail made by his horse which he had left hobbled three or four hundred yards away.[16]

After the hardships of the trail, Mexico City, with its French restaurants, *cotelettes à la milanaise* and Burgundy wine, should have provided a civilised change for Gabrielle (and less so Robert), more accustomed to the fine living of Paris. But even Mexico City in those days was an "unhealthy place to ride in after dark, without your navy colt." Graham describes to West one experience he had there:

In those days right in the middle of the town (of Mexico) there was a little park full of trees and crossed by sandy paths. Riding across it one evening on my black horse, without my rifle but with a mother-of-pearl handled Navy Colt round my waist and another dangling from the saddle horn, a gentleman suddenly appeared out of the wood, and edged his horse towards me. I observed with pleasure I was the better mounted of the two. Seeing that I had drawn my pistol he reined up at about 20 yards away. Then taking off his hat he asked me what o'clock it was. Still covering him I answered. "Just on the stroke of six". He thanked me, wheeled his horse and disappeared into the trees.

And all these details remembered fifty years after the event. Surely a tribute to Graham's memory — or his imagination.

Tschiffely would have us believe that Graham, finding that the price of cotton had dropped, had to sell his load at a loss. Whether this be true or not, the Grahams certainly found themselves in the position of having to work at least part of their two months in Mexico in order to support themselves. Graham, we know, served as a fencing master at an academy there (his certificate, made out in the name of Robert Bontini, is still preserved), whilst Gabrielle apparently taught French and painting at a girls' convent school. Presumably they devoted some time to seeing the sights of Mexico City, for at Chapultepec Castle they came across the eight captive survivors of the Mescalero massacre that Gabrielle describes in "The Waggon-Train." Despite his non-idealistic view of the Indians, Graham was so moved to pity by their plight as to immortalise them in one of his best Mexican sketches, "A Hegira."

After two months in Mexico, the Grahams decided to head back for San Antonio by the same route, a journey that was dogged all the way by the epic trek of the Indian prisoners who had escaped and were also making their way home to their territory in the Santa Rosa Mountains. The inhuman treatment of the warriors by the white settlers was to impress Graham greatly for the rest of his life, as one sees not only in his politics but also in his writings. By May 1880 the Grahams were safely back in San Antonio; the Indians, murdered to the last child, were not so fortunate. In the want of correspondence during the fifty-two day return journey, "A Hegira" is as valuable a commentary for the trip home as Gabriela's sketch of the waggon train was for the outward journey.

By 28 May 1880 Robert was writing to his mother:

> We have just got back. The journey was not so bad as going, and we passed through some lovely frontier country on the other side of the Rio Grande. . . San Luis Potosi I like better than Mexico City, for it is a very curious old town. However, the people are most disagreeable, and to me it is very unpleasant not to be able to go outside a town alone. In nearly all parts of Mexico it is too dangerous to do so and every one travels in company of ten or twelve, at least, all well armed. San Luis Potosi is especially dangerous. . . Everything is very quiet here. No Indian or Mexican raids, lynchings, elections, negro agitations or anything. Not even a revolution in Mexico. In fact nothing worth mentioning except a riot in our good town of Monterey between the police and the military, in which after a horrible [?] battle that lasted a few hours, most of the police were killed. But I understand that there has been no novedad since & all is serene. . .

But on the whole Graham quite liked San Antonio. Many years later, far removed from the passion and the excitement of the moment, in a letter to Herbert West, dated 16 April 1931, Graham gives us a more objective view, perhaps even coloured by the distance of memory, of how it was in the 1880s:

> San Antonio was my town, though a different San Antonio from today. I used to unsaddle always at the Buffalo Camp and then make my way to the Menger Hotel, where I had a trunk of store clothes. Then, I fancy, there would be a schooner of beer, a cocktail or a whisky straight, for Texas was a free country in those days, and certainly a thirsty land.
>
> We used to say talking of the great drouth [?] in "a thirsty land," that land is Western Texas.
>
> A Prohibitionist would not have been a popular citizen in the "Santone" of those days.
>
> They were the days of the Mexican freighters, buffalo hunters, cowmen, and other worthies of whom the world was not worthy. . .[17]

Between July 1880 and his departure from Texas early the following spring Robert was engaged in various activities, though his letters, as Watts and Davies have also observed, are "remarkably reticent about his actual work" (p. 48). In fact, one can almost see a pattern in Graham's correspondence before and after the Mexican waggon trip. The pre-waggon train letters are full of interesting comments on the American way of life, people, climate, events, etc., with *occasional* references to happenings back home in Britain. The post-trek correspondence from July 1880 to April 1881 is much more concerned with British and world news, politics, literature, theatre and the like. Perhaps he was already beginning to realise that the Texas venture was not turning out as profitable or as satisfactory as he had hoped, and now he was preparing himself for the inevitable return home — hence the constant talk of positions, contacts, money, business interests and so on, in Britain.

But by early June 1880, just after his return from Mexico, this was not yet the case. He was, we know, involved in a ranching partnership with a Mexican-Greek with whom he had set up a property near the Mexican border ("a week's hard riding from San Antonio," according to both Tschiffely and Watts/Davies). During Graham's absence on a business trip, the ranch was the object of an Indian raid, which left the homestead devastated and the cattle spirited off. Since all their capital had been invested in the ranch, the young couple were, if not down to their last $100, as Tschiffely tells us, at least in serious financial straits.[18] Although his letters home over the next six months were just as regular, there is little evidence as to his employment — or his penury. Apparently he was engaged in several buffalo-hunting trips, acted as an interpreter, and also participated in several cattle-driving sorties between Texas and Mexico and back.

His trips apparently took him away from home to many regions beyond Texas, in New Mexico and Arizona, where he is supposed to have schooled horses. On one of these excursions he met Buffalo Bill at the Horsehead Crossing, a famous meeting confirmed by Don Roberto himself in a letter written many years later to Teddy Rossevelt (27 March 1917), quoted in the sketch "Long Wolf," contained in this volume. Although Tschiffely had a great affection for Don Roberto, and we can forgive him many lapses of strict adherence to the truth as a result of his hero-worship, he does strain our credulity somewhat by asking us to believe that on one of these treks across the plains Graham just happened to meet a solitary rider who turned out to be his old friend Pancho Pájaro from his youthful days on the Argentine pampas a decade before.[19] Meanwhile, it seems, Gabrielle, left alone in Texas during her husband's forays in the South-West, had returned to New Orleans (their first stop in the New World), and was again teaching painting and French at a convent school for girls — activities consistent with her tastes and talent, gifted as she was in both of these areas.

Perhaps due to his commercial failures, and probably out of nostalgia for the halcyon days of his youth, it would appear that Graham had had enough of abortive ranching schemes, cattle-driving and horse-grooming in Texas. In response to two letters which he had received in Texas earlier in the year from his old friend George Mansel, who had invited him to invest some of his capital in a ranch partnership with him in the Argentine, Robert decided to join his friend there. By 20 August 1880, and apparently having been there some time, he was writing to Gabriela from the Estancia de las Arias, República Argentina, apologising for not having written sooner, and praising this region as a charming part of the country, followed by a detailed description of the ranch and the surrounding area:

> I wonder how you can still stay away [with] those odious Yankees in Texas when down here it is much nicer & we might have such horse and ostrich hunts, also deer hunts together. If you can come, just drop me a line by what steamer you are coming & I will meet you at the Hotel de Provence calle Cruz also with a tropilla of horses & we will sally out.[20]

Signed "Roberto el Gaucho," it adds the P.S. "Mind and bring Jack [their dog] with you."

Since Gabrielle chose to stay with the "odious Yankees," the frustrated gaucho was obliged to return to Texas and rejoin his wife. The rest of his stay there seems to have been uneventful, if we are to judge by the correspondence. The books that his mother had been sending him occasionally during his North American stay are mentioned several times — the classics like Shakespeare, *Don Quixote*, the *Golden Treasury*, *Gil Blas*, moderns like Huxley on Hume, Scottish writers like John Galt and, appropriately, Bret Harte. Names are dropped casually and easily in his more frequent discussions of British politics — Randolph Churchill, Disraeli and Gladstone, who was to be his first party leader and prime minister on Robert's election to Parliament for the Liberals in 1886. There are occasional references to American politics (Garfield, Hancock), civil war in Mexico, and presidential abdications (not to mention absconding with public funds), but remarkably little about his own life and activities in San Antonio, in the letters of July, August and September.

One letter to his mother, dated 10 October [1880] contains a rare personal reference — viz. that he had had a riding accident, which he underplays in his usual self-effacing manner. Political events of the time are treated and dismissed equally flippantly: "the coloured population of Lynchburg have just hung a Baptist minister. . . Sitting Bull the Sioux chief after being converted by a Universalist missionary has just had him scalped. . ."

Another letter from his friend Mansel in Argentina arrived 29 November via Graham's mother and must have cheered him up, although reminding him of his own commercial ranching failures. Realistically accepting his slim chances of obtaining a consulship or a Queen's messengership, he re-echoes his initial impressions of Texas (in a letter dated 21 October 1880): "I am getting more reconciled to Texas. Mexico is a much nicer country but I hate always being boxed up in a town as one is almost forced to be there.''

With the sad news of his grandmother's death, and the fading chances of a consulship, Robert consoles himself (in a letter dated 12 January 1881) with looking forward to a trip to La Habana, to escape the malaria brought on by the heavy rains. But ten days later in another letter to his mother (22 January 1881) he confesses regretfully: "I am not going to Tampico or the Habana as the journey costs too much and Yellow Jack [fever?] is at Tampico, I believe.''

Obviously suffering from ill-health and growing indigence, Robert was cheered somewhat by a visit from his brother Charles in the spring of 1881. Charles' letter to his mother of 1 April 1881 bespeaks a good time, riding, learning to throw a lasso, and generally seeing a great deal of the country under Robert's expert guidance. But it seems obvious that Charles had ulterior motives for making the long journey. Robert's health was not in good shape. His financial condition was even worse. After a series of business disasters — he had long overdrawn his family allowance — and bad health (riding accident, kidney trouble, malaria) it was evident that Robert needed help. Charles was clearly the emissary from home bringing good tidings, and promise of monetary help. In a postscript to Charles' letter (1 April 1881), Robert, with a mixture of resignation and relief, writes to his mother: "How jolly it will be in Spain & not in the least resembling Texas." With this brief epilogue, the Texas adventure was over.[21] Robert and Gabrielle went straight to Vigo in Galicia from San Antonio, having arrived at La Graña by May 1881. They were to stay in Spain off and on for the next two years, supported by yet another generous allowance from his mother.

Mrs. Bontine never quite accepted Gabrielle into the family, and it is possible that the allowance was increased so that he might stay abroad and not bring his wife home to Britain. The hope was, perhaps, that he would learn to live within his means as a "gentleman of leisure" and not invest his much-needed capital in harebrained commercial schemes, as he had done in the River Plate and later in Texas.

With this quiet voyage from New Orleans to Europe, Graham's Texas stay was over. Though not the most successful two years in his life (materially or physically), it gave him an opportunity to see the Northern continent, and to confirm his views on man's inhumanity to man that he had first observed on the plains of Argentina. After an initial period of adjustment, it strengthened his humanitarian outlook and his opposition to bigotry and racism, cruelty and exploitation, which were to be the bases of his political career in another five short years. Not less important, it provided him with the material for, if not his most fertile literary period, at least an important part of his artistic formation, as the following sketches will demonstrate.

The Text

Though not as fecund as the South American part of his life, then, the Texas, Mexico and South-West U.S.A. stint provided some very interesting pieces. It was here that he first articulated his desire to work some of his experiences into articles, although he did not feel too confident about the end result: "I have tried two or three times to make a magazine article out of the Mexican journey, but find I have no talent whatever in that line. . . I think I have no literary ability whatever" (letter to his mother dated 3 July 1880). Looking at some of the spelling and punctuation (not to mention the barbarous handwriting), one is not surprised. However, within a decade Robert was writing irate, but interesting, letters to newspaper editors, prefaces to other writers' works, travel and political articles for magazines, book reviews, etc., many of them based on these very North American adventures.[22]

Most of the sketches published here appeared first in periodicals prior to their book publication, which usually took place within a year or so of the periodical appearance. Since Graham often amended and polished up the book version, I have chosen the first edition form as the more up-to-date, complete and carefully edited version. Graham's lack of concern with frivolous details like proof-reading and correcting is now legendary.[23] In terms of selection, there are, I suppose, two anomalies. The first piece, as the title indicates, is not a sketch, but my compilation or correlation of three virulent letters that he wrote in the space of a few weeks to the *Daily Graphic* on the barbarous treatment of the Indians in Dakota. They seem to me so important for his views on the Indian problem, and as some of the earliest examples of his vitriolic prose, that they merit not only inclusion, but also their important position as a point of departure for the North American sketches.

The other anomaly is the inclusion of Gabrielle's "The Waggon-Train," which is such a detailed description of their life together on that journey from San Antonio to Mexico City that one could not hope to improve on it. This sketch highlights, in a way that Graham himself never spelled out, the daily chores, details of organisation, not to mention the day-to-day dangers of the trail that *he* took for granted. It also helps to complement the little that Robert wrote about this trip — apart from "A Hegira" — and supplies us with much information not otherwise available, since the correspondence of this period is demonstrably thin and scanty.

In my grouping of the sketches I have adopted several criteria for the arrangement. I have tried to bear in mind the chronological order of writing, so that we may have some idea of the evolution of Graham's prose, since these pieces were published over a long period between 1890 and 1932. Whenever possible I have maintained the order of date of publication. But I have organised the material to give something of the chronological passage of their two years in North America, i.e. their travels from New Orleans to Brownsville, San Antonio, Monterrey, San Luis Potosí, Mexico City, back to San Antonio,

Robert's trips to New Mexico, Arizona and other parts of the South-West, before their final departure again from New Orleans to Europe. With this in mind I have also arranged the sketches geographically in a way that will reflect the different excursions and visits, all the while attempting to reconcile *my* order with the dates of publication. Fortunately, there are very few cases in which the chronological and the geographical clash so violently as to destroy the artistic content or contradict the narrative/biographical process.

I have chosen to start with Graham's "Three Letters on the Indian Question" not just because they are some of the first examples of his writing, but also because they act as a strong point of departure, and as a focus for a flashback to his life in North America, which leads to his later philosophical standpoint. I have elected to conclude the volume with an extract from Graham's sketch on Tschiffely's famous ride from Buenos Aires to New York, which duplicates that part of Graham's own odyssey from Mexico back to San Antonio. Appropriately, Graham leads us back along the same route that he and Gabriela had followed fifty years before. This is conversely apt, since five years later Tschiffely was to repay the master by describing Graham's adventures of a half century before in his *Don Roberto* biography of 1937 in the wake of Graham's death. There is a kind of Borgesian aptness in this circular repetition of events — my using the same material that Tschiffely employed to write about Graham, who had already treated the epic ride of Tschiffely, who was to follow the same route as Graham, who also described his future biographer's adventures . . . ad infinitum.

Given the spread in time of the pieces contained in this collection, part of my editorial task has been to impose some kind of stylistic consistency in the sketches with regard to spelling, grammar and other formal details, like quotation marks, parentheses, accentuation, capitalisation, etc. In many cases I have omitted capitals, italics, etc., in certain words that Graham had used, if I consider the word so common now as to be acceptable in standard English. Obvious orthographical and typographical errors, both in Spanish and in English, have been corrected. Punctuation, as his early correspondence indicates, can sometimes be a problem with Graham. Whenever necessary, I have judiciously inserted, or discreetly removed, a comma, semicolon or a period in the interest of clarity, but only after much deliberation, because Graham's prose is so evocative and so personal that what looks like bad grammar (for example, a missing verb) is often his own special brand of rough poetry, which reflects much of the character of the man, reflected in his impressionistic writing.[24]

Since these are sketches about Mexico, Texas and South-West U.S.A., there are, of course, many allusions to American and Mexican history, politics, literature and customs. For the benefit of the general reader I have supplied explanatory footnotes. For those linguistic matters not explained in the notes I have also provided a glossary. Although many of the words will be familiar to American readers, especially from those regions of the United States treated in the sketches, the function of the glossary is to help others to a fuller enjoyment and appreciation of Graham's colourful sketches. Thus it is perfectly clear that the glossary is not intended to be exhaustive, specialist or technical, but a mere guide to the interested reader.

Although, as I indicated in the Foreword, there has been a renewed interest in Graham, and some of his work is now in the process of being reprinted, the original first editions are now rare items and difficult to obtain. I have, therefore, supplied a check list of Graham's writings, plus a select list of books, articles and bibliographies on his life and works, especially as they pertain to his stay in Mexico, Texas and South-West U.S.A. (1879–81), which may help readers to pursue their interest in a writer who is slowly being rehabilitated. These North American sketches provide not only a fascinating picture of a way of life now long past, but also reveal much about Robert Bontine Cunninghame Graham, the man and the writer.

NOTES

1. George P. Isbell, "Cunninghame Graham in Texas," *Southwestern Historical Quarterly*, XLIX, No. 4 (April 1946), 501-09.
2. I have consulted all the Guernsey letters to Graham (1901-06).
3. See for example his reviews, "An Unknown World," of Carl Lumholz's *Unknown Mexico* (1903) in *Saturday Review*, 96 (19 December 1903), 757-58; "Mexico," of C. R. Enoch's *Mexico* (1909) in *The Nation* (London), 6 (10 July 1909), 535-36; "Porfirio Díaz," of J. F. Godoy's *Porfirio Díaz* (1910) in *The Nation* (London), 7 (16 July 1910), 568; "Impressions of Mexico," of H. Baerlein's *Mexico, the Land of Unrest* (1913) in *The Nation* (London), 13 (9 August 1913), 720-21; "Mexico," of Mrs. Alec Tweedie's *Mexico* in *English Review*, 25 (December 1917), 509-14.

   See also his letters to the press, e.g. "Mr. Cunninghame Graham and the Apache," *Saturday Review*, 88 (21 October 1899), p. 521; "Mexico and President Díaz," *Glasgow Herald*, 15 May 1911, p. 521; "Slavery in Mexico," *Glasgow Herald*, 29 May 1911, p. 5.
4. See "A Page of Pliny," in *A Hatchment* (1913).
5. See, for example, his sketch "Niggers" in *The Ipané* (1899) for a bitter indictment of Britain's role in nineteenth-century world affairs.
6. Letter from Graham to H. F. West dated 24 July 1931, partially reproduced in West's 1932 biography, pp. 47-49.
7. I have operated from the original letters, most of which are now preserved in Harden, the home of Lord and Lady Polwarth. When unable to read Graham's writing, I have also consulted parts of the published versions of some of the other brave souls who have tried to decode Don Roberto's perverse hand, viz. West, Tschiffely, Watts/Davies, and Lady Polwarth.

8. See my article "Cunninghame Graham: Una nueva perspectiva crítica," *Revista Canadiense de Estudios Hispánicos*, IV, No. 2 (Winter 1980), 218-24.

9. I have tried as far as possible to leave the quotations from the letters as they were originally written, unusual spelling, punctuation and all, since they indicate something of the man, and point to certain stylistic characteristics that were to emerge in his published writing. I have, of course, omitted parts of the letters that do not pertain to the subject at hand. These omissions are indicated by my ellipses.

10. Horses.

11. Although he never mentions her in his correspondence home to his mother. Watts/Davies comment on this too (p. 41).

12. A pun translated roughly thus: "If this is the Body of Christ, where is the soul of the lawyer buried?"

13. "These oxen are all the possessions I have, and this dear little bull is like a daughter to me."

14. Tschiffely's reproduction of this letter (p. 147) contains a parenthetical interpolation that does not exist in the original letter: ("You must remember I have my wife with me"). Tschiffely, of course, edited much of Graham's correspondence, but usually through omission, not addition. One wonders if Tschiffeley, in his reading of the correspondence, had noticed the lack of references to Gabriela, and had inserted this parenthesis as a kindly gesture so as not to highlight the absence of Gabrielle's name from the letters. Or could it have been a suggested addition by Graham himself (who collected and reread the letters) for posterity?

15. Tschiffely has the 19 January and the 6 February letters mixed up, as if they were both one and the same letter.

16. Part of this letter was also reproduced by West in his biography (pp. 47-49).

17. Parts of this letter were also reproduced by West in his biography (p. 265). For some strange reason he omitted the sentence referring to Western Texas as "a thirsty land."

18. In spite of an allowance of £400 per annum, by the time the Grahams left Texas in the spring of 1881 their debts amounted to £2000 (Watts/Davies, p. 48).

19. See the sketch "La Tapera," in *Progress* (1905). This could, of course, be another stretching of the imagination by the subject of the biography himself to provide grist for the mill of Tschiffely, who received from Graham only the information and the papers that the latter saw fit to hand over. It certainly contributes to the legend of Don Roberto.

20. Neither West nor Tschiffely nor Watts/Davies mention the Argentine episode at all, which is surprising, although it has been indicated and confirmed for me by Lady Polwarth. Perhaps Watts/Davies do not mention it since they quote a 21 August letter (of Robert to his mother) from San Antonio as 1880 to give proof of Robert's illness. This, of course, cannot be reconciled with a 20 August [1880] letter from Argentina. If one accepts the 20 August letter as proof of his visit to Argentina in 1880, then one can only infer that the 21 August letter from San Antonio re his illness is of 1879.

21. George P. Isbell, in his aforementioned article in the *Southwestern Historical Quarterly*, has Graham still in San Antonio in 1882, although there is no proof of this elsewhere. In accordance with Tschifelly, his main source, Isbell has Graham and his wife leaving for Scotland in 1883 to be home with his critically-ill father. Isbell goes one step further, and has Graham back in Texas by the end of 1885 or the beginning of 1886 after his defeat in a November 1885 election. Since Graham was subsequently elected to Parliament shortly afterwards in July 1886, the second visit hardly seems likely, and is not corroborated by any other source.

22. See Cedric T. Watts, "R. B. Cunninghame Graham (1852-1936): A List of his Contributions to Periodicals," *The Bibliotheck*, Vol. 4, No. 5 (1965), 186-99.

23. See, for example, Conrad's letter to Graham, dated 9 December 1898: "You haven't been careful in correcting your proofs. Are you too grand seigneur for that infect labour? Surely I, twenty others, would be only too proud to do it for you. Tenez vous le pour dit. I own I was exasperated by the errors. . ." Also reproduced in *Joseph Conrad's Letters to R. B. Cunninghame Graham*, p. 111.

24. Graham, of course, was well aware of all these "defects" in his writing. In the Introduction to *Rodeo* (1936), Tschiffely's omnibus anthology of Graham's sketches, the master with characteristic irony describes himself thus: "But still I might have finished all those sentences; not broken off to moralise right in the middle of the tale; split less infinitives, and remembered those rules of grammar that I have disregarded, as freely as a democratic leader tramps on the rights of the poor taxables who put him into power" (p. xvi).

EDITOR'S PREFACE

The three letters on the Indian question, which were first published in the *Daily Graphic* in 1890-91, are interesting from the point of view of content, style and chronology. They were all published at the height of Graham's political career (1886-92) at a time when he was contributing letters and articles to the press, both lay (*Pall Mall Gazette, The Speaker*, etc.) and socialist (especially *The People's Press*) on matters of great social import.[1]

H. F. West printed them in garbled and incomplete form in his 1932 biography (he had no date for the third letter) and Tschiffely reprinted them in his 1937 biography, perpetuating the errors and the missing date. C. T. Watts lists the first two letters in his valuable "R. B. Cunninghame Graham (1852-1936): A List of his Contributions to Periodicals," *The Bibliotheck*, Vol. 4, No. 5 (1965), 186-99. I have managed to find the missing date for the third letter, and have restored all three to their original pristine "purity," based on the published pages of the *Daily Graphic* for the respective dates.

I think the correlation of the three letters produces a much more powerful document, the whole being an anguished cry from the heart against the cruel treatment of the American Indian from a humanitarian who had learned his lessons first-hand on the plains and hills of South-West U.S.A. Written in 1890-1891, the letters reflect something of the concern he had expressed in his letters back home to his mother a decade before.[2] This barbarous treatment of the Indian by the white American was to be rendered in much more artistic terms in an authentic literary sketch, "A Hegira," a decade later.

The co-ordinated letters serve as a potent opening, and convey something of the influence that his North American experience had had on him. Translated into political terms, they are a clear manifestation of his social and humanitarian concerns at this period. Artistically, they are a good point of departure to reconstruct not only his North American past but also his literary recreation of that past which will transcend mere chronological and geographical frontiers. That surely is one of the tests of true art.

NOTES

1. See my articles, "Voices of Socialism: R. B. Cunninghame Graham," *Tribune*, 29 April 1966, p. 14; and "R. B. Cunninghame Graham and *The Labour Elector*," *The Bibliotheck*, Vol. 7, No. 3 (1974), 72-75.
2. See for example the letter dated 1 November 1879 quoted in my Introduction, pp. 11-12.

THREE LETTERS ON THE INDIAN QUESTION

The American Indians: Ghosts Dancing[1]

The special correspondent of the *Sun* at Pine Ridge, Dakota, keeps us informed of the movement of the Indians now massing their forces at Cherry Creek.

Glancing over the evening papers we see that the Sioux are dancing the Ghost Dance, and learn that in the opinion of the perspicacious correspondent the settlers expect to be robbed and murdered. Some of us may say, "Confound these Indians, they ought to be shot down". Yes, smokeless powder is your true civilizer after all. There is no good Indian but a dead Indian, which we know is true, for have not American humourists declared it, and has not a tender-hearted public in two continents affirmed their declaration with a laugh. Artists wish they could be present to see the ceremony. Those who, in pursuit of money, have been in the "Territory", the whisky sellers, the Bible pedlars, the land speculators (having caught the phrase from some frontier man), tell us "Indians is pizin", and, like Peter, seal the lie with an oath. The general public glances over the telegrams from Omaha and hopes that there will be no bloodshed, then turns to discuss the recent political scandals and the prurient details connected with the private life of party leaders, which, of course, we all know are of vastly more importance than the extermination of legions of heathen Indians. Still, there are few who really realize what is going in the snow at Cherry Creek, what the Messiah really is the Indians are looking for, and who the ghosts are who are dancing. A Ghost Dance to the Sioux is what the Holy War is to the Mohammedan, what the Last Prayer (faith present or faith absent) is to the Christian. The Sioux can stand no more; therefore, they are dancing to the ghosts of their forefathers to arise and help them against their enemies. Only an Indian superstition. Looking for a Messiah. Waiting for the Las Casas who will never come.[2]

I wonder if the British public realizes that it is the Sioux themselves who are the ghosts dancing. Ghosts of a primeval race. Ghosts of ghosts who for three hundred years, through no crimes committed by themselves (except that of being born), if it be not a crime to love better the rustle of the grass than the shrieking of the engine, have suffered their long purgatory. Ghosts who were men. The Messiah these poor people are waiting for, our poor people here in London also look for. But both will look in vain. Justice will not come either to Cherry Creek, no, nor yet to Whitechapel. The buffalo have gone first, their bones whitening in long lines upon the prairies, the elk have retired into the extreme deserts of Oregon, the beaver is exterminated to make jackets for the sweater's wife, the Indian must go next, and why not, pray? Is he not of less value than the other three? Let him make place for better things — for the drinking shop, for the speculator, for the tin church. Let him realize that in the future, where he changed his peltries for beads and powder, two gills of whisky shall be sold for a quarter. Men say the change is good (but good is merely relative), perhaps good enough for him, but death, indeed, for all ghost dancers.

Civilization, perhaps, one day will remember them when the civilized Indians, [whom] commercialism is creating, are dancing around the flames of European capitals.

But Rocky Bear and the Little Wound, Short Bull and Sleeping Water have had enough, they have taken horse, mounting lightly as drops of water (from the offside) silently, in single file, never stopping but to squat and pass the pipe round; each man holding his pony by the mecate, they are marching on Cherry Creek. But the Kiowas, the Cheyennes, the Arapahoes, the Comanches have braided their horses' manes. They (who before civilisation loved one another as the dwellers in Liddesdale and Bewcastledale did of old)[3] are friends.

They have mounted their best horses, they are coming through the day, they are coming through the night, across the frozen prairie (the dry grass hardly crackling beneath the bronchos' feet), they are passing the whispering red woods, coming through the lonely canyons, marching silently as ghosts on Cherry Creek, across the lands that once were theirs to take counsel with the ghosts of those their former owners.

Better that they should come and smoke and dance, "dance for ten days without food or water", better far that they should die fighting, than by disease and whisky. Outrages they will commit, of that there is a certainty, but all they do can scarce atone for all that they and theirs have suffered. Tricked by all, outwitted, plundered by the Christian speculator, better far that they should die fighting, and join the ghosts who went before them. This I want the world to recognise, that even Indians do not contemplate their own extermination without centuries of suffering. We might have taught them something, they might have taught us much, soon they will be all forgotten, and the lying telegrams will speak of "glorious victories by our troops". Once more sin will be committed in the name of law and progress. It is a hard case to decide on, no matter from what side you approach it; these men have lived too long, better, therefore, they die fighting. No one will regret them (but myself) — except, perhaps, their ponies, who may feel their new owners' hands heavy on the horsehair bridle. The majesty of civilisation will be vindicated, one more step towards universal hideousness attained, and the Darwinian theory of the weakest to the wall have received another confirmation to strengthen those who want to use it against the weakest here in Europe.

Salvation by Starvation: The American-Indian Problem[4]

The first act in the concluding drama of the existence of the Sioux Indians is played out. Apparently, in direct violation of the President's express orders, the Indian police arrested Sitting Bull, with the natural consequences that a rescue was attempted and a fight took place. In the fight, Sitting Bull, who was heard giving his orders in a loud voice, fell pierced by a bullet. This is an old trick, well known in Spain and in Mexico, and throughout the frontiers of the United States.

The escort appears at the frontier town without the prisoner. Officer reports prisoner endeavoured to escape, and, in the struggle that ensued, was accidentally shot. Quite so; that is to say one of two things happened — either the prisoner was offered a supposititious occasion to escape, and shot in the attempt, or else he was deliberately murdered in order to save time, legal expenses and the problematical Spanish-American or Uncle Sam's justice (sic).

This would seem to have been the end of Sitting Bull — deliberately murdered to stop him asking for food for his tribe. "Minds" in Boston's "first families", in the south, and that noxious product of civilisation, the Anglified American, the man who secretly laments that there is no peerage in America, will talk of Lutz and Pijano.[5] The editors of Western papers will talk of the safety of the settlers being at last secured by the removal of Sitting Bull, and worst of all, the American public as a whole will believe them, and think a piece of poetical justice has been performed.

Poetical, no doubt, but as for justice — as far removed from anything connected with it as was the other specimen of American "justice" executed three years ago in Chicago,[6] and for the self-same reason, namely, that the culprits asked for bread. American justice! American justice to Indians, above all, is a minus quantity. American justice to anyone who dissents from the gospel of cent per cent means the bullet or the gallows; to the Indians it has meant starvation or the bullet. What wonder that they should have chosen the bullet?

Still, it is a cheering thought that most of them (I hope not Sitting Bull) have been baptised, and that their souls will be saved, though their bodies have been starved by the Christian American Government.[7] Sitting Bull was right in his life-long policy that the whites are the mortal enemies of the Indian race.[7]

Whether in Patagonia, on the pampas, or on the prairies of the North West, the treatment that the whole Indian race has received, whether at the hands of Spanish or English Americans, is a disgrace and a scandal even to that disgrace and scandal facetiously called civilisation, — in which the doctrine of whether the iron pot strike the earthenware pot, or the earthenware pot float against the iron pot, fuel for the earthenware pot has become a gospel.

Every one who knows the Indians seems united on one point — that the recent disturbances are due to starvation and to the deliberate witholding of the covenanted rations from the wretched Indians. As Mr. Moreton Frewen says in the *Pall Mall*: "Theirs (the Indians) was the cattle (the buffalo) on a thousand hills. Theirs was the whole country, the prairie, the woods, the rivers, and they were free". It would seem — and I speak not as a sentimentalist who takes his Indian (coloured) from the pages of Fenimore Cooper,[8] but as one who has passed many a night staring into the darkness watching his horses when Indians were about; it would seem that food were a little enough thing to grant them in their own country. True, I am one of those who think that the colour of the skin makes little difference to right and wrong in the abstract, and who fail to see so much difference between an Indian sitting over a fire gnawing a piece of venison, and a tailor in the East-end of London working in a gas-lit den sixteen hours a day for a few shillings a week. It does not much matter, though the bulk of mankind declare that a prairie with corn growing on it, and a log house or two with a corrugated iron roof, is a more pleasing sight than the same prairie with a herd of wild horses on it, and the beaver swimming in every creek.

That is their opinion, and they will not, I am sure, deny me the right to express mine, that, as the Spaniards say, "Hay gustos que merecen palos" (There are tastes that deserve sticks).[9]

But the gain to civilisation. You would not surely allow these rich lands to remain for ever in the hands of a few wandering savages? Again, I say that to me the mere accident of a little more colouring matter in a skin does not alter right or wrong and that the land was theirs, no matter to what uses they put it, centuries before the first white man sneaked timidly across the Atlantic.

Those who are loudest now (the settlers in Dakota) for the final extermination of the Sioux fail to grasp that, when Dakota is all settled, they themselves will in the main become as dependent on the capitalists as the Indians now are on the United States Government, and that the precedent of rigorous measures with the starving Indians will be used against themselves.

I would, even at the eleventh hour, secure the Indians in a fertile territory, and prohibit any white man from settling among them, except he were a man of proved good character.

I would in that territory make it a criminal offence to supply drink to any Indians.

I would exclude all missionaries except those of the Roman Catholic faith, for in my experience of missionaries and Indians the Roman Catholics alone have seemed to me to understand them.[10]

Lastly, I would endeavour to set up cattle ranches among them, for in my experience of Indians this is the occupation to which at present they are best suited.

My frontier friends may smile at my idea of Indians as ranchers, and exclaim, with expressions which I spare your readers, that the Indians would eat all the cattle in a week. All I can say is, I have seen the Indians in the Gran Chaco, and on the frontiers of Chile, no whit less savage than the Sioux, make first-rate ranchers when drink was away. At least we owe the men from whom we have taken their all, replacing doubtfully the beaver and the buffalo with whisky and smallpox, some reparation beside a small-bore bullet.

Even in America, where public opinion is, perhaps, more brutal than in any other country of the world, surely a flush of shame must rise to the faces of honest men when they receive the telegrams from Dakota. It puzzles me to think, except the horse, what benefit the Indian race has gained from civilisation.

Perhaps, though, it is better that the evil should come quickly, for it will come at last. In the next generation or so they will be gone, and then the Americans will organise picnics on a grand scale to visit the historic places in Dakota and Montana, where the curious and picturesque peoples (*vide* advertisement to cheap circular trips from New York to Dakota) "who once inhabited our continent, lived and smoked their red calumets."

The Redskin Problem: "But 'Twas A Famous Victory"[11]

"Our special correspondent" at Pine Ridge, Dakota, whose despatches I have read with such heartfelt pleasure for the last month, has had the opportunity lately of assisting in one of the most healthy manifestations of the spirit of civilisation that it has been the lot of any special correspondent (out of Africa or Egypt) to chronicle for many years. I freely admit I am dense, and density is as the sin of witchcraft, but be that as it may, I never yet was able to discover why it is, when a body of white troops, well armed with all the newest murderous appliances of scientific warfare, shoot down men whose ignorance of proper calling clearly proves them to be savages, the act is invariably spoken of as a glorious victory. There are some things which be too hard for me, and the way of the serpent on the rock is as easy of comprehension in comparison to it, as is the fact that the particular political party to which I choose to belong is composed of upright, righteous living, whole-souled patriots, and that the other fellows are all either rogues or fools, or an amalgam of the two.

If, though, the previous fact is difficult of comprehension to me, how much more so is the converse fact that, if the aforesaid braceless, breechless knaves, in precisely the same manner, shoot our "glorious troops", their proceeding become a "bloody massacre", a "treacherous ambuscade", or something of a low-priced nature of that sort.

I should have thought that sauce for the Indian savage was also sauce for the white rowdy who swarms in all frontier corps, even if the latter worthy was acquainted with the priceless boons of boiled shirts and plug hats, and worshipped his fetish in a stifling meeting house instead of on the open prairie. Still, that in no wise alters the case that there has been a glorious victory of the American troops at Pine Ridge. Very pleasing to read that after three centuries the good old racial feud between Indians and whites is being fought out in the good old way.

Let it be once granted that there is no good Indian but a dead Indian. Does that apply, though, to Indian women and children? I see that our "brave troops" remorselessly slaughtered all the women and children, and our special correspondent, in estimating the "bag", remarks that by this time probably not more than six children remain alive out of the whole Indian camp.

Can anything more miserable be conceived than the forlorn position of the wretched Indians, when at the break of day they found their camp surrounded by troops, when, at the same time, we remember they were probably half-starving, and that the recent severe weather is as summer compared to the winter of Dakota.

I cannot imagine anyone reading (always from our special correspondent) and not feeling the profoundest pity for the wretched Indians. The spectacle of them sitting silently in a semi-circle, one would have thought, would have appealed to anyone but an American frontier soldier. We are told that the Indians planned an ambuscade, but it would seem a curious kind of ambuscade that 120 men should allow themselves to be surrounded by 500, backed by artillery. That many of the Indians — now so fortunately dead — had murdered settlers and fired ranches I have little doubt. That the whole Indian question (like the question of the unemployed in London) is a most difficult and piteous one no one will deny. Still, though, hardly anyone who knows Indians can refrain from thinking that in this instance there seems to have been a deliberate attempt to goad them to fury in order to shoot them down. Any old Indian fighter will agree with me that to attempt to deprive Indians of their arms by surrounding them at daybreak with troops was certain to produce a conflict. The Indian resents nothing in the world like an attempt to deprive him of his weapons.

He is almost born with them. His little bow as a child grows with him, becomes strong and tough with him, and is buried with him. It is no more his fault that generations on generations have been accustomed to go armed than it is the fault of a mustang, born a pacer, to refuse to trot.

It is as ridiculous to expect an Indian to love work as it would have been to expect a Highlander of the time of the '45 to take to typewriting rather than cattle-lifting as a means of subsistence.

Indians will (and experience, both on the pampa and prairie, has taught me this) only deliver up their arms at a time of solemn treaty or in the presence of an overwhelming force. Five hundred men were enough to destroy, but not enough to overawe, one hundred Indians.

No one should have known this better than the officer in command of the troops. Therefore, I believe the whole affair was arranged beforehand by men who knew perfectly well what would happen. One's very soul revolts in disgust from the account of the cruel butchery, the shooting down of fleeing savages with Gatling guns, the useless and cruel slaughter of the women and children.

The only consolatory feature of the whole affair is that the Indians seem to have fought like demons and inflicted severe loss on the troops before they were exterminated.

I had hoped that the matchless pen of Bret Harte[12] would have raised a protest against the doings in Dakota; if the protest had been made it would have run through the American press like wildfire, and surely must have produced some good. Soon, I suppose, we shall hear of some more glorious victories of the same kind, and then the ghost dancers can all dance together in some other world, where we may hope there may be neither Gatlings nor any other of the pillars of civilisation to annoy them.

It seems a pity, too, to waste so many good Indians who might have been so advantageously used to turn honest pennies for enterprising showmen, if no other method of utilising them occurred to the great American Republic. However, I may be permitted to make my moan over the women and children at least, for I doubt much if they had committed any weightier crimes than the unpardonable one of living.

Now that they are dead they will furnish an excellent repast for the coyotes; and, for the Indians, they would have died hereafter; and, after all, what does it matter? For, as Montaigne says, "Quoi, ils ne portaient pas des haults de chausses".[13]

NOTES

1. First published in the *Daily Graphic*, 29 November 1890, p. 14.
2. Bartolomé de las Casas (1474-1565), Spanish coloniser turned Dominican friar who, because of his life devoted to the native American, earned the title of "Apostle of the Indies."
3. Graham is referring to the traditional rivalry and border disputes between Scotland and England, as represented by these two towns on either side of the frontier, in Roxburghshire and Cumberland respectively.
4. First published in the *Daily Graphic*, 22 December 1890, p. 6.
5. In fact, although the original newspaper edition says "Lutz and Pijano," both West and Tschiffely have "Cortés and Pizarro."
6. This bitter indictment of American justice was omitted by Tschiffely in his biography. Graham is referring to the Haymaker Riot (4 May 1886), prompted by a confrontation between police and strikers over the Eight Hour Movement. Bombs, allegedly thrown by anarchists, killed seven people. Of eight anarchists arrested and tried, four were hanged after a trial that many people considered a farce.
7. Both West and Tschiffely omit this touchy passage criticising American attitudes towards matters racial and religious.
8. James Fenimore Cooper (1789-1851), American novelist, who wrote on the clash between the old frontier way of life and approaching civilisation in novels like *The Pioneers* (1823), *The Last of the Mohicans* (1826), *The Prairie* (1827), *The Pathfinder* (1840), and *The Deerslayer* (1841).
9. In the original newspaper edition it appears thus: "There are tasks that deserve stocks" — a comment on Graham's barbarous handwriting!
10. West, touchy as ever about religious matters, added a footnote here in his biography to explain that Graham's experiences were confined to South America, Mexico and South-West U.S.A. This view of

missionaries, and in particular his praise of Catholic ones, Graham reiterates throughout his work. Cf., for example, *A Vanished Arcadia* (1901) on the Jesuit reducciones in Paraguay, and sketches like "A Jesuit" in *Father Archangel of Scotland* (1896).

11. First published in the *Daily Graphic*, 5 January 1891, pp. 5-6, this is the letter included by both West and Tschiffely, but without date.

12. Francis Bret Harte (1836-1902), American writer of Western short stories like "The Luck of Roaring Camp" and "The Outcasts of Poker Flat." During the 1880s he was United States consul in Scotland, and spent the rest of his life in London. Graham would have known him in both places. In the collection of Graham correspondence housed at the National Library of Scotland, Edinburgh, there is a letter from Harte to Graham dated 28 November 1890, on this very Indian question, in which he states: "Of course the desire to "improve" people off the face of the Earth with a gun, and then to punish them for learning how to use the weapon will continue to exist." It is not a coincidence that Graham wrote his virulent letter to the *Daily Graphic* just weeks after receiving this letter from Harte.

13. Michel de Montaigne (1533-92), French essayist and philosopher, author of several books of *Essais* — the first two published in 1580, the third in 1588. This sentence, the correct version of which is: "Mais quoy, ils ne portent point de haut de chausses" meaning "Why, they don't even wear high boots!" is taken from Montaigne's essay "Des Cannibales," Book I, Chapter XXXI.

Graham was a great admirer of Montaigne, of course, and it is rather interesting, and a rare tribute, that his friend Frederick R. Guernsey (in a letter dated 26 October 1901) should equate them thus: "I give my homage to Montaigne and Cunninghame Graham for masculine and stimulating reading."

EDITOR'S PREFACE

"Un Pelado" is one of the earliest of Graham's sketches on the Texas scene. The fact that it appeared in *The Ipané*, which contains some of Graham's most scathing attacks on man's inhumanity to man, indicates the mood and tone of the story. It was apparently based on a newspaper cutting that had been sent to Graham five years after he left Texas (Watts/Davies, p. 45). In his sketch Graham attributes the report to the San Antonio *Evening Light*, although, in fact, as Laurence Davies demonstrates in his unpublished article "No Sense at all: Cunninghame Graham and a Texas Hanging" (*c.* 1973), it appeared in the San Antonio *Daily Express* of 16 January 1886. George P. Isbell, who had Graham back in Texas in 1886, claims that this is the "first printing of any story that has been definitely authenticated as his own." It is very difficult to take this theory seriously since Graham, it has been proved, had left Texas as early as 1881 and had never returned. Also, the fact that he was fighting and winning an election in July 1886 makes the possibility of his being in Texas at this time highly unlikely.

Isbell had, of course, another theory that Graham was also responsible for a series of notes from Gaza's Crossing in the *Evening Light* during the summer of 1882. Quoting the *Evening Light* of 30 June 1882 ("A young Scotchman speaks of the endurances of his Buenos Aires horses in comparison with the Texas stock"), Isbell is convinced that Graham was the author of several other Gaza's Crossing columns in the *Evening Light*. Davies, in his aforementioned unpublished article, argues that it is *possible* to take this claim seriously on stylistic grounds. But, it should be noted that at the time of writing this article Davies had Graham leaving Texas in 1883, and not 1881, as we all now agree. If Graham did write the 1886 *Express* report, his stylistic hand is not strikingly obvious. To have written both would have involved him in a clever manifestation of self-parody.

What is clear from "Un Pelado" is much more of the bitter irony and satiric observation that were characteristic of Graham's other writing at this time (1897), e.g. the biting attacks on the Scottish character that one finds in the naturalistic "Salvagia" and "A Survival," the companion pieces to "Un Pelado," which were gathered together in *The Ipané*. The bitter lessons of the Texas experience, for example the racial bigotry, had not been lost on Cunninghame Graham.

UN PELADO[1]

Not far from where the Old Comanche Trail crosses the Nueces lies the little town of Encinal in Western Texas, county of La Salle, upon the International and Great Northern Railway track. A little one-horse place, just where the post oak country touches the great open but mesquite-covered prairies of the south. Oak forests to the north, oak and more oak, as post oak, "black jack," live oak, with hickory, pecan, red bud and hackleberry; bottoms rich and alluvial in which grow cotton; bayous alive with alligators; woods, woods, and still more woods, right up to Texarkana, on by Nacogdoches, and from thence to Little Rock and the Hot Springs upon the Arkansas. To the south the prairies stretching to the Río Grande, once open grassy seas, when the Comanches and Lipans burnt them every spring, as sheep farmers in Scotland fire the heather, but now all overgrown with chaparral, composed of dwarf mesquite and sweet flowering guisache, low-growing ahuehuete intermixed with cactus, till nearing the great river, the very Nile of North America, all vegetation ceases, and salt plains replace the scrub-grown prairie, and at last even the salt grass vanishes and a stone-covered sandy waste serves as a barrier between the rival states.

The town itself a helot[2] amongst cities, and contrived, apparently, to fill the double object of showing what a town should never be and of example to the world at large of how much uglier a modern mushroom town can be than an encampment of the Diggers or the Utes.[3] Frame-houses made in the North, then numbered in pieces and railed South, and put together like a Chinese puzzle, shingles for roofing, and each dwelling raised on blocks after the fashion of a haystack. No shade, no trees, except a straggling China tree or two in the sand waste known as the plaza. A tramway running down the thoroughfare called Constitution Street. A coloured Baptist church, a second Presbyterian ditto, and the cathedral, half of adobe and half of "rock," conveyed at great expense from Goliad[4] by the members of the Pioneer faith, as Roman Catholics are styled in Texas. Three bar-rooms known as saloons, a bank, some stores, in which all kinds of notions, from "ladies' fixings" down to waggon grease and coal oil, were on sale, and where hung quirts, Mexican bits and horse-hair reins, with cinches, Winchesters and white-handled pistols for cowboys on the spree. Before each house a horse, tied by a lariat and saddled with a high-peaked saddle, with a rifle hanging to the horn, stood sleepily.

Horses in every street, in every yard, in waggons, buggies, hacks; mares hitched to Milburn waggons, with foals running at their feet. Horses asleep right in the middle of the plaza; horses that strayed about like dogs in an Oriental town and seemed to have no owner; some tied to posts, apparently asleep, till an incautious stranger passed too near, when, with a squeal, they bounded from the ground and stretched their lariats quite taut, till the strain slackening they plunged against the post, like boats left at a stair and bumping on the steps as the waves rise and fall.

Nothing aesthetic in the whole town, and still the people not without the attraction that energy imparts. "Cleargritted" to a man, shooting "plum centre," riding a "pitching" horse as if they were Indians, free-swearers, proof against all kinds of drink, not civilised and yet not savages, voting the Democratic ticket straight, and determined to uphold what they thought justice, especially when "niggers," Mexicans, or Indians transgressed their code.

Across the creek straggled the quarter of the Mexicans known as Chihuahua. Entering its purlieus, one came upon another world. The houses either made of adobes, or else mere huts, a cross between an Indian "wickey-up" and a Mexican jacal, were made, as nests of prairie dogs are made, of everything that came to hand. Kerosene-tins and hides, sides of stage-coaches, ends of railway cars, with all the wreckage of a prairie town, were used in their make-up. Still they seemed adequate for men in blankets to lounge against and plan what they could steal. Wrapped in serapes, overshadowed by poblano hats, their feet encased in high-heeled riding-boots, and in their eyes a look of half good-natured villainy, the population stood confessed a rogue. Few worked, all owned a horse, a game-cock, and every self-respecting man on feast-days went to play monte in a building lettered "Restoran and Koffe." So Encinal sat facing its suburb, the two destined, like man and wife, never to understand each other's motives though living side by side. In Encinal the people, go-ahead, commercial men, but yet idealists like all the members of the Celto-Saxon race, determined to deceive and be deceived on all those points which the uneducated and slothful Mexicans in the suburb of Chihuahua perceived quite clearly and acted on like true materialists. In Encinal, Sunday, with all its horrors of closed shops, the "bell punch" in the bar-rooms, and an air of gloom congealed the town like a black frost at each week's end. Across the creek it was a holiday, with cock-fights, races, and an air of merriment which in itself went far towards atoning for the past week's villainy. On one side, moral citizens, under cover of the night, slipped when they could up to the "mansions," mysterious, strongly fenced in, and solitary houses on the bluff which all the day looked dreary and deserted, and by night were all lit up, and flared with the electric light, which of course found its way to Encinal, whilst Paris, London, and Berlin still clung to gas. But still, these stealers to the "mansions" in the dark were moral men, because on Sunday they all sat in church ejaculating "Hallelujah!" or joining in the responses audibly, according to their creed.

No one was moral in Chihuahua, or made the least pretence to be. If men disliked their wives, they took another to help them bear their cross; and if a wife found that her husband treated her unkindly, she too looked round and cast her eyes upon some able-bodied unconnected man to help her bear her woes. Still, in Chihuahua the women understood woman's first duty — that is, to be a woman — more clearly than the elliptic print-clothed "females" or elaborately arrayed "white ladies" in the town of Encinal.

But as mankind is ever wont to typify, making the virtues feminine, the vices (if I mistake not) male, calling the Spaniard proud, the Italian treacherous, the Frenchman fickle, and so on, and understanding best what a town, country, race, or what not, is like by summing up his, their, or its characteristics in some man, I do the same.

Therefore, I take José María Mendiola and G. M. Hodges as prototypes, both of Chihuahua and of Encinal. The one a Mexican, working at what is called freight-hauling in the United States, that is what we should style a waggoner. The other station agent, and a keeper of a local store. Both rogues, but different in degree, and each unable to discover any taint of virtue in the other's life.

José María, long, brown and thin, his lank black hair showing his Indian blood, his furtive eye and nervous hands all proving him to be what the Americans, for reasons not explained, refer to as a greaser.

Hodges, a "real white man," fresh-coloured with the sandy hair and clear blue eyes which mark the man destined by Providence to keep a shop.

Just how the thing "kim round," as Texans say, no one was ever sure.

Some say that Hodges cheated Mendiola about a pistol, and others that José had swindled Hodges about some bill. That which is certain is, that in full day José María "filled Hodges up" with bullets from a Winchester that he had borrowed from the man he shot. Sheriff McKinney of Cotulla took the murderer, and twelve citizens, all in due course, brought in the verdict "murder in the first degree."

What follows, the reporter of the San Antonio *Evening Light* shall tell.[5]

"Justice in Encinal: conviction against José María Mendiola, one of the Mendiolas of La Salle, a low-down crowd of 'greasers', located between Cotulla and Encinal.

"The victim's brother travels from Jacksonville to see José turned off, says that he guesses he would have come ten thousand miles to see the man who shot poor Gus buck in a horsehair rope. He complains of the accommodation in the 'sleepers' on the third section of the 'doodle-bug', and remarks he guessed he almost lost the 'round up' after all, as 'road agents' held up the car in which he travelled, at the long switch in the 'perara' outside Vermillionville. After a drink I started out to interview 'our Mary', as you might call José María. Found him quite chipper, mighty peart, and sassy as an Indian pony on the young grass, smoking a loud cigar. María allows that he was raised at Las Moras, Kinney County, Texas. Has no record of his birth, but guesses he is twenty-five. Was reared in Western Texas and says: 'I have always lived there, never lived nowhere else. I have never wanted to live anywhere else. No wife, *sabe*, therefore no children to mourn for me. Old man and mother still both living near

Encinal; sisters, brothers, two or three will see me die. I reckon they will also see I am not afraid to die.'

"As he said this, he drew his blanket (called it a serape) round his shoulders and shivered, for it was a mighty piercing norther, and he was dressed like most pelados in cotton fixings, all except his blanket.

" 'Yes, señor; I have no trade, but little education, speaky no English. Understand him? Yes. All my life I have been a hauler, with a mule-wagon.'

" 'Home influences?'

" 'No, señor; very poor Mexican. Have drunk some mezcal — not very much — too much. Yes, I killed Hodges; he took my ivory-handled pistol.[6] He swindled me, and I shot him.

" 'What do I think of my sentence?

" 'There is no justice in it. If there was any justice anywhere they would not take my life on the thing they are building out there. All the proceedings were in English. I did not understand a word. They told me I was to be hung. I said "Bueno". Curse your Corregidores; curse your Courts! No, I am not religious; born a Roman Catholic, but am a Universalist; think all religions should get a fair show. That saw and hammer go all day, only at night I get some rest. *Sabe*, eh? They finished the scaffold and pulled it down again because it was not quite level. Oh, these Americans; what does it matter if it was level or not? Even the earth is not quite level, for a poor man, very poor Mexican.'

"This let me out [remarks the talented reporter] and I lit for the Maverick House, and after some 'Rock and Rye', sat down to think about what I had heard. I allow that Mendiola was, like most picayune 'greasers', really a fatalist, reckoned he had a Kismet or a something which predestined him to do the deed. Anyhow, he is not the first citizen of La Salle who has gone up the golden stair with the assistance of a half-inch rope.

"Back at the Maverick House — all over now. José María just turned off. He looked pale, but showed grit, and in a neat-fitting black suit (Dollar Store cut) made an elegant appearance. One of the most singular features of the whole show was that there was little swearing or ribaldry amongst the crowd; even the Aztecs, who had turned out in force, some coming from Carrizo Springs the night before, and camping in the plaza, seeming not much excited. Father Kosbiel, a Polander, had 'corpse' in charge. José stood mighty quiet, and as the City Marshal finished reading the warrant, slightly shrugged his shoulders and said 'Muy bien.' The reverend father then performed the offices for the deceased, and turning to the people said: 'Citizens of Encinal and of Cotulla, this poor Mexican, who stands beside me, will shortly stand before his God. He asks your pardon, and regrets that he can speak no English so as to express to you that he is penitent, but he humbly asks for the sympathy of all men as one about to die.' The reverend father seemed much overcome, but Mendiola remained unmoved, and merely saying, 'Adiós, Padre,' stepped on the scaffold, and in an instant was jerked into eternity. 'Dead,' said the physician, 'in four minutes.' The people gossiped awhile, unhitched their horses, and then dispersed. I guess María Mendiola was a stupid animal, but he showed 'clear grit' right to the end. Father Kosbiel says he died a Catholic, and that the manner of his going showed his trust in God. Dunno, guess he said he was a Universalist, but any way he seemed the least concerned of the whole outfit, and looked as if he would be thankful when the affair was done."

Thus far the reporter, but an aged settler, as the shavings flew from his pocket-knife and whittling stick, pronounced the epitaph: —

"No sense at all," said he, turning towards the nearest saloon; "just didn't have no sense at all. Like killing a goat, didn't have sense enough to be afraid."

NOTES

1. From *The Ipané* (London: Fisher Unwin, 1899). Originally published in *Saturday Review*, 83 (15 May 1897), 535-37.
2. An enslaved or exploited person or group. The helots were a class of serfs in ancient Sparta, halfway between slaves and free citizens.
3. The Diggers were a short-lived egalitarian group who began in 1649 to cultivate English common lands as a protest against government exploitation. The Utes were a group of Shoshonean peoples of Colorado, Utah and New Mexico.
4. Goliad, a small town in southern Texas, was seized by Texans at the start of the Texas Revolution. In 1836, when the Mexican advance began, Colonel J. W. Fannin and three hundred men were shot during an attempted retreat. Hence the Texans' cry at San Jacinto: "Remember the Alamo! Remember Goliad!"
5. It was in fact the San Antonio *Daily Express*. See Editor's Preface, p. 35.
6. "It is the ambition of every Texan and most Mexicans to own either an ivory-handled or a mother-of-pearl handled pistol. It gratifies them just as much as a baronetcy does a successful sweater, and is more readily compassed by the poor in spirit" (Graham's footnote).

EDITOR'S PREFACE

"Un Pelado" conveyed something of the dangerous life of the frontier, the lawlessness and the bigotry that existed between the Texans and the Mexicans on the other side of the Río Grande. As today, the Mexican immigrant worker, legal (*bracero*) or illegal (*wetback*), was a feature of the 1880s, and Graham met many of them on his travels and during his working experiences as a novice businessman in his early months in Texas. He was to have other dealings with them on his return from Mexico and the unsuccessful cotton enterprise.

Miguel Sáenz, a native of Chihuahua, was one of these Mexican emigrés. A storyteller, sage, "man-of-no-work,"[1] he had substituted the guitar for the knife and the gun, although he never forgot how to use the traditional weapons nor his equestrian skills which he had acquired as a frontier rider and a reluctant revolutionary. Now he preferred to devote his energy to watching the girls. As a frontiersman, he never lost his healthy fear of the Apache Indians, although they were a very rare sight around San Antonio in the early 1880s when Graham lived there.

NOTES

1. A. F. Tschiffely in *Rodeo*, his 1936 anthology of Graham's sketches, renamed this piece "A Philosopher."

A CHIHUAHUEÑO[1]

No one, at first sight, would have taken Miguel Sáenz for a man born on an Indian frontier, or for one who in his youth had handled arms.

Short, fat, and looking as if he had been cut by an unskilful workman out of walnut wood, he wore a faded black cloth jacket and the bed-ticking trousers which so many frontier Mexicans affect. A wide and steeple-crowned poblano hat, stained here and there with perspiration, and girt with a heavy, sausage-like band of silver tinsel, sat like a penthouse on his head and overshadowed the whole man. His occupation in fine weather was to stand against the wall of his jacal wrapped in an Indian blanket, and criticise adversely the horsemen of the village as they passed, whilst not neglecting to put in a word or two more favourable as to the charms of all the girls, and speculate on those their clothes veiled from the public gaze. His business was to play on the guitar, and sing to melancholy accompaniments in do minor, wailing jarabes treating of love disdained, of Indian battles, and of the prowess of celebrated horses, for he was músico, that is to say, by strength of wrist and perseverance, and with the natural advantage of being a little deaf, he had arrived at some proficiency in what he styled his art.

As he sat nursing his guitar, and with a bland yet cunning smile upon his pock-marked face, no one would think that he had been a frontier rider, and that still, though his abdomen overhung the pommel of his saddle, that, once upon his horse, he was fixed there as firmly as a knot upon a tree. He looked out on the world through his black, wrinkled, and Indian-looking eyes, tired with surveying miles of prairie for hostile "sign", and gazing out intently into the night against attacks by the Apaches, indulgently, being aware of all its frailties and his own. "Trust not a mule or a mulata wench," he would observe, or "If a woman is a harlot and gets nothing for it, she might as well remain respectable," with other adages of a like cynical and primitive philosophy formed half the staple of his talk. These he enunciated with so much unction and such gravity that they appeared to be not only the epitome of human wisdom, but the high-water mark of his own personal experience, which he retailed half humorously, half sadly, for the behoof and guidance of the listeners, and as a sort of vade mecum to mankind.

"Weapons are necessary," he used to say, "but no one knows exactly when; therefore, your knife should come out easily, and pistol locks be kept well oiled, for fear of novelty." "Never go up to a jacal where dogs are thin, for he who does not feed his dogs will starve his guest," he used to say, as with an air of having proved his statement by experience.[2] "In entering chaparral, note if the birds sit quiet on the trees, for if they fly about, be sure some one has recently passed by, and on the frontier all are enemies till they have proved themselves as friends, and so of life." "Waste not your graces on a deaf man," and "amongst soldiers and with prostitutes all compliments are held excused," and "who shall say it is the post that is at fault if the blind man did not observe it in his path," were of the flowers of his rhetoric which he bestowed upon a listening world after a glass or two either of sweet tequila or mescal.

Born in Chihuahua and having migrated up and down the Río Grande from the Pimería to Matamoros, and wandered with the Indians in his youth in the Bolsón de Mapimí[3] and from Mojave to the Río Gila, fate had at last brought him up in a backwater of frontier life in San Antonio, Texas, where, in the quarter called after his native town, he sojourned, waiting the time when he should find himself in funds to return home and end his days in peace.

In the meantime, and because, as he himself averred, it was not good for man to live alone, he had taken to himself two wives, and induced peace between them by frequent beatings, till, as he said, they learned to love each other and live in charity and with the fear of God.

Outside his hut, built like a bird's nest, with canes and wood, and roofed with empty tins of kerosene, his saddled horse all day stood nodding in the sun, and when his master had occasion to repair in his capacity of *músico* to any merry-making, he mounted, getting to his seat as actively as in his youth, all in one motion, and taking his guitar from one of his attendant spouses, struck a slow lope, holding his instrument balanced on his thigh, and with the diapason sticking out after the fashion of a lance. "Don" Miguel Sáenz — for, as he used to say, not only was the title his by right, but in Chihuahua the treatment was universal in the province — had, besides proverbs, much lore of Indian battles and of revolutions, which on occasion and with circumstance he would unpack.

Then as he sat immovable with his right hand stealing occasionally behind his back to assure himself that his revolver was in place, his dull unblinking eyes would suddenly become illuminated, and as he talked of battle, murder, rape, and sudden death, you saw the Indian blood assert itself and the inherited ferocity of centuries shine in his face, and then in spite of rusty black cloth coat, fat stomach, and ill-tuned guitar, that "Don" Miguel was not, as he would have expressed it, "one of those mules that a man can drive before him with the reins."

In early youth he had been taken up and forced into the ranks by some "pronouncing"[4] general in Chihuahua, and his adventures in the revolutionary campaign, which led him up and down over the plateau of Anáhuac, furnished him with ample anecdote and opportunity for the indulging to the full of that quiet philosophic cynicism which is the characteristic of all those Mexicans who have a strain of Indian blood.

"Soldiers and harlots," he would say, "are much alike, each give their souls for money, and their love and hate are swift, and dangerous as a tiger's leap; therefore be friends with them as if you shortly might be enemies, and do not give your arm for them to twist, or they will break it in the socket, and then laugh. Have you not seen an Indian mother catch a rabbit or a bird, and give it to her children to torment? See how she shows them how to put out its eyes with thorns, and break its wings, in order that their hearts may become steel, and that their souls may suffer others' tortures and their own, without a tear."

War in Chihuahua and Sonora, before the advent of "Don Porfi" to the presidential throne,[5] was not a kindergarten. No one surrendered who was not weary of his life, for if he did, the Indian mother's lessons usually made his death a boon to him. Marches were desperate in the keen air of the high plateau, and the infantry was lashed along behind the cavalry by officers with bare machetes in their hands. Those who fell out never fell in again, for, to encourage those who kept the ranks, they were incontinently shot, or if a foolish sentimentalism saved them for a time, their death was certain if a picket of the enemy came on them, even supposing that they did not die of thirst like baggage animals who sink beneath their packs.

With a cruel humorous twinkle in his eye Miguel would tell how, when the troops came to a water-hole, a guard was set to keep the over-driven infantry from drinking till they burst.

Once, as he said, when sitting on his horse, worn out and thirsty, certain men annoyed him overmuch by importuning him to be allowed to drink.

Troops, as he said, learn only by experience, so he determined to make experiment on some of them for the good guidance in the future of the rest. Beckoning up two or three, he let them drink, which they did heartily, lapping the icy water with their fevered tongues. In a few moments they were seized with violent pains, and in a little time lay down and "died like doves" quite quietly, so that in future no one bothered him when he sat tired on his horse guarding a well.[6]

"Our Saviour gave His life for all, and I, Don Miguel Sáenz, not being born a saviour, yet saved the life of many a good soldier merely by giving this example, that is in their own persons, for discipline is as the soul of military men, and if the body perish, let but the soul be saved and all is well."

And as he said it he would chuckle fatly, and the villainy of a fat man has something unnatural and bloodcurdling, and acts upon one, as the speech of Balaam's ass, which must have been more disconcerting to its rider than all the antics of a buck-jumper.[7]

For foreigners in general he had the easy tolerance and contempt of all inhabitants of South and West America, reckoning them up as men who cannot ride, and therefore are not to be taken seriously. For North Americans, whom he termed *los gringos*, his feelings were more mixed; the western and therefore riding section of them, in his eyes, were worth consideration when on their horses, but their rough manners and want of knowledge of the world — on foot — induced in him an attitude half pitiful and half contemptuous. The northerners, who throughout Texas are termed "men from the States," he looked on as a man convinced of witchcraft might look upon a wizard, half in alarm, mingled with loathing, and yet with admiration of his power and wickedness.

Spaniards he called *los gachupines*, and probably had never seen one, but seemed to think them a sort of dragons roaming about, politically inclined, scheming by night and day to take away that liberty which so few Mexicans enjoy, but which each one of them imagines that his fathers shed their blood to consecrate. Speaking himself a harsh old-fashioned jargon of Castilian, plentifully garnished with Indian words, he yet had his own theories as to diction, holding that gachupines whistled like the birds, that Germans cried, and that *los gringos* spoke as if attacked by syphilis.

Los indios bravos sat like a nightmare on his mind, although in San Antonio, Texas, they were as rare as they would be in Liverpool; but having heard their war-cry in his youth, it had remained for ever in his ears, as men blown up in mines, in after years, are said never to lose a singing in their heads.

"The Indian," he said, "is such a kind of beast; you cannot kill him with a stick or stone." The animals [are], as is well known to all philosophers, created solely with a view as to the easiest way a man can find of killing them. "The Indian dies hard, and when you have him wounded on the ground, do not approach at once, for no coyote better can feign death. Therefore stand still and fire upon him as he lies, twice, thrice, or even four times, until you see no twitching of the limbs when the ball strikes him. Even then be cautious, and, having lit a cigarette, keeping your eyes upon the body all the time, advance with your gun cocked, and, on arriving at the carrion, drive your knife two or three times into the heart. Then he is dead and you can glorify the Lord and take his scalp." No self-respecting frontier man, Yanqui or Mexican, who did not in those days conform to the Indian custom, as far as scalping went; and though they spoke of Indians as "savages," or as *los bárbaros* (according to their kind), themselves were to the full as great barbarians as any warrior of the Lipans, Comanches, Coyoteros, or of the Mescaleros, who dug for roots of wild mescal along the shores of the Río Gila or wandered in the deserts of the Mapimí. So that the listeners who heard the Chihuahueño's counsels of perfection as to Indian fight, were not surprised, but testified their admiration at his wit and his "hoss-sense" by a sententious "bueno" or "jess so", according to their nationality, for to all frontier men no Indian was ever good, till he was well filled up with rifle bullets. Still, in his heart of hearts, the ex-Indian fighter, now turned half-pimp and half-guitar player, rather admired the Indian though he feared him, in the same way that a fat white housekeeping shopkeeper in the East admires the Arab of the plains.

Both frontier Mexican and Eastern shopkeeper seem to see their vices and their virtues typified, and, in some measure, purified by the wild life led by their prototypes. So may a politician reading Machiavelli bring his hand down violently upon the book, and say, "This was a man indeed: to what heights might I rise if I could only frame my lies with such intelligence."

Thus would the Chihuahueño chuckle long when he read or heard of some successful Indian raid, so that it did not touch his native village, which he referred to always as *mi tierra*, looking upon it as the centre of the earth.

"Yes," he would say, "I see the thing and how it fell about." Likely enough the idiots saw a herd of horses feeding on the plain, and did not see the lumps upon their backs, which were the feet of Indians clinging to them. So they allowed them to approach, and then each horse turned a *centauro* in a moment, and they all were slain except the women, who would be carried off to work in the tepees.

Books did not bulk too largely in the Chihuahueño's mind, though what he read became a portion of himself, never to be forgotten, and to be commentated on, as something which the whole world knew, just as it knew of sun and rain, of change of seasons, and the precession of the equinoxes.

The old romance called the *Twelve Peers of France*[8] he had, bound in grey parchment, and lettered on the back by someone who preferred his own phonetic spelling of the names to the mere trifling of grammarians. It read, "Istoria de Carlo Mauno y los dose Pares."[9] On Carlo Mauno would he often talk, saying he held him for the chief of emperors, being, as he was, a valiant man, and having killed most of the people that he met — a view of the imperial function perhaps more suitable to the meridian of Baghdad than of Mexico.

"Alejandro el Mauno" with his horse Bucefalo came the next in his esteem,[10] and from his story he would draw sage apothegms and rules for life, which gave him great consideration amongst such of his compeers as could not read, or, at the best, had learned laboriously to spell out a prayer in Latin pronounced like Spanish, and but little understood.

Riding, apparently, amongst the Greeks, held quite as high a place in public estimation as in Chihuahua, for it appeared a king owned Bucefalo, and, as there was no heir to the throne, put out a *bando*, offering the crown and his fair daughter's hand to the successful rider of his horse. All the *jinetes* came from far and wide, each with his *cuarta* in his hand, his legs enclosed in *chaparreras*, and wearing silver spurs which made a noise as when a hailstorm falls upon a roof.

But "el caballo Bucefalo" bucked so hard that he despatched them all at the third jump, leaving them *mal parados*[11] and with their "baptism half broken", causing them all to swear abominably, and making some of them in their disgust desert their faith and go and join the Turk.

Then apeared Alejandro, not yet El Mauno, but, as it soon was seen, with indications of his greatness, for he had armed himself for his attempt with a great bit, which weighed half an arroba, and his spurs were of the size of the tops of oil jars, all of solid plate. When Bucefalo saw his armament, he straight gave in, and Alejandro, mounting at a bound, raced him up to the king, and, stopping him, caused him to rear, so that he hung suspended for an instant over the very throne. This pleased his majesty, who at once took the bold rider to his heart, marrying him incontinently to the princess, who was wonderfully fair, and should have made him happy, but that the love of other women caused him to fall from grace, and lose eventually his kingdom and his life.

It fell in this wise. As it so chanced, the Grecian state happened to be at war with Persia, whose king was Dario,[12] and whose daughter (name unknown) was also passing fair. After the victory, in which both Bucefalo and El Mauno performed prodigies of valour, cutting down Moors as if they had been grass, and taking many scalps, it chanced that Alejandro in his tent, being athirst, called for the Persian princess to bring him one of those beverages which those infidels affect. She, having put a potent poison in the cup, brought it to Alejandro, who straight drank, and instantly swelled out enormously and ultimately burst. "Thus do we see," the Chihuahueño said, "how that the love of women is a curse, and, reading history, you may light upon things that are useful to a man as guides in life."

His learning and his skill on the guitar, together with his fund of anecdote, made him a favourite in the society in which he moved, and his companions would lament that, though he had two wives, he yet was childless, and that no son would fill his place when he slept with those Chihuahueños whose souls are twanging their guitars in paradise. A shade of sadness sometimes obscured the twinkle in his eye, when he would say, "No, señor, children I have none, neither by Carmen nor Clemencia. No Christian boy will close my eyes when they have put the *baqueano*[13] in my hand."

Then pensively, and with an air as if his life had had its sweetness and its charm, he used to say, "I had a son once in my youth, born of an Indian woman, a Mojave squaw, who should by now be grown to man's estate. *Barajo!*[14] the little rogue, son of an Indian harlot, he must have taken many a Christian's scalp by this time if he has turned out such a devil as his dam."

NOTES

1. From *Progress* (London: Duckworth, 1905). First published in periodical form in *Saturday Review*, 96 (25 July 1903), 107.

2. This is a favourite saying of Graham. He often used variations of it in his Argentine sketches to make the same point.

3. In the original text the accent is misplaced. This is interesting, and perhaps typical, because Graham actually took the trouble to write to his American journalist friend in Mexico City, Frederick R. Guernsey, who in a letter (dated 30 April 1904) spells out the correct version. Either Graham forgot, was too careless to follow up his inquiry, or was badly served by his editor. Knowing Graham's attitude to correcting and proof-reading, the third explanation is less likely.

4. That is, issued a *pronunciamiento* or a call to arms, inviting a military uprising. This is still a popular way of precipitating a change of government in Latin America and, as we have seen recently (1981), even in Spain.

5. Porfirio Díaz (1830-1915), dictator of Mexico from 1876-1911 before being overthrown by the rebellion initiated by Madero that was to culminate in the Mexican Revolution.

6. Another favourite Graham anecdote quoted elsewhere. Even Gabrielle includes it in her story, "The Waggon-Train."

7. In the Book of Numbers the prophet Balaam was saved by his ass, through which God spoke. By disobeying the Almighty the prophet would have been killed by an avenging angel, if God had not reproached him through the ass which Balaam had beaten.

8. *Les Douze Pairs*, or the Twelve Peers of France, including Roland and Oliver, were warrior companions of the eighth century Frankish emperor Charlemagne. They figured in the various *chansons de geste*, and especially in the twelfth century epic poem *La Chanson de Roland*, in which Roland and Oliver were defeated and killed by the Moors at Roncesvalles Pass in the Pyrenees, as Charlemagne arrived too late to save them.

9. The phonetic spelling can be translated as "The History of Charlemagne and the Twelve Peers."

10. Alexander the Great, King of Macedonia, 4th century B.C., and his famous horse, Bucephalus.

11. Absolutely stunned or confused.

12. Darius I, King of Persia, 5th century B.C.

13. "*Baqueano* means a guide; hence the consecrated wafer is the great *baqueano*, as it leads to heaven" (Graham's footnote).

14. Euphemistic variation of the swear word "Carajo!" usually translated as something mild like "Dammit!" or "Hell!"

EDITOR'S PREFACE

In the Introduction I suggested that "The Waggon-Train" was an anomaly in the sense that it was not written by Robert, but by his wife Gabrielle. However, since it describes in detail an important part of their life together in Texas/Mexico, I think its inclusion is not only justified, but desirable. Gabrielle's description may be simple, even childish, as Graham admits in his preface, but is such a true and authentic version of life on the trail at that time that it merits publication.[1] Also, it fills the gap in Graham's own correspondence at this time, and is one of the few sources of information for this period, about which Graham wrote comparatively little.

It was Graham, after his wife's death in 1906, who arranged for the publication of this piece and other tales, plays, translations, etc., in *The Christ of Toro* (London: Eveleigh Nash, 1908), as well as *Rhymes from an Unknown World* (London: Duckworth, 1908). Her *Santa Teresa: Her Life and Times* (London: A. & C. Black, 1894) came out in a new edition in 1907 (London: Eveleigh Nash). She also contributed three pieces to Robert's *Father Archangel of Scotland* (London: A. & C. Black, 1896).

"The Waggon-Train," then, written in 1880 when she was only twenty, is one of her earliest published works. If lacking the strong philosophical and mystical qualities of her later prose and verse, it is a useful piece of nineteenth century travel literature which contributes to Texan-Mexican customs and lore, and is a valuable source of information for the life of the young Grahams at this period.

NOTES

1. One of the obvious stylistic defects is her constantly changing tenses, often for no apparent reason.

THE WAGGON-TRAIN[1]

by

Gabriela Cunninghame Graham

Preface by R. B. Cunninghame Graham

This collection of sketches [The Christ of Toro] *includes "The Waggon-Train," a description of a journey made in the year 1880, when the writer was only twenty. The life she writes of in it has passed away.*

The journey, which took us over fifty days from San Antonio de Bexar, Texas, to the city of Mexico, is now made in three. On the Río Grande, where then the Mescaleros, Jicarillas, and Lipans wandered, the trail is now haunted by no greater dangers than is the road from Jaffa to Jerusalem. Still at times it seems to me, when waking suddenly at night, that it is well to stretch my hand out to feel if rifle and six-shooter are within easy reach, and not infrequently (such is the force of habit, Postume!) I catch myself wondering if my horse is tied securely, for he seems unnaturally quiet, upon his rope.

Well, well! the simple narration of the journey, written almost in a childish way, but still so truthfully that when I read it I feel compelled to start up on my feet and say, "Yes, yes; that was the day the Indians sacked the town of Juárez," or, "That was the place where we came through the village of the prairie dogs," I now submit to those who must perforce read it without the stimulus of memory. After all, who shall decide if memory or hope gives the most pleasure, or whether each of them is but a mere anaesthetic to dull the pain of life?

The waggon-trains which go from San Antonio de Bexar (Texas) to the interior of Mexico, present to the European or the Yankee from the Northern States a sight sufficiently curious. The waggons are large and solidly built, with ponderous wheels, and covered with tilts of white canvas to protect the merchandise from the weather. They are capable of carrying an enormous burden, and may be considered as being the ships of the Mexican deserts, as they are in fact. Each waggon is drawn by a team of from ten to twenty mules, harnessed in two rows of four abreast, with a couple of wheelers, one of which is ridden by the driver, whose traps and necessaries for the journey dangle over the wheels or from the back. These consist of cooking utensils, ropes for mending broken harness, and spare boots with bright red or yellow tops; whilst his rifle is carefully slung in front, near at hand, ready for immediate use. Underneath, beside a hammock which he scrambles into when tired, runs the four-footed guardian of all this property, a lean, mangy cur — the object of his master's solicitude and the constant sharer of his fortune. The amount of capital required to run one of these mule-trains would seem astonishing to a European, but the risks are great and very often the profit precarious. The country to be traversed is sometimes bare of grass for hudreds of miles together, and hay or some other kind of fodder, as well as corn, has to be carried. A mule's ration of corn is about twelve pounds a night. The men (always Mexicans), if good steady workers, receive twenty dollars a month and their food. Both the sailor on his voyage and the muleteer on his journey are obliged to live in a state of enforced sobriety.

Muleteers resemble sailors in many respects, though [those of] one class pass their lives on the sea and the others in the wilds. On arriving in port — and a Mexican frontier town is a kind of desert port — both too often spend their wages, that have cost them so dear, in a few days' space. Sometimes both classes desert, and the ship or waggon-train goes out short-handed.

The muleteers usually manage, before starting on a trip, to have as much of their salary advanced as possible, upon various pleas. Some leave this with their wives and families, should they happen to have them, but most spend it in dissipation.

Often, at the moment of starting, the majordomo has to hunt up his men through the different gambling dens and drinking shops, or to bail them out of the lock-up, as they usually manage to get into trouble, and perhaps stab some one.

The excitement is unbounded as we leave San Antonio, "outward-bound" for San Luis Potosí; and it reminds one forcibly of a vessel clearing out of London docks. Men say good-bye to their wives, children, and sweethearts, or shout and swear fiercely at the restive mules; dogs bark, and the mule-boy, a sort of savage, brown and ragged, his hair coming through the crown of his ragged, silver embroidered hat, and iron spurs on his dilapidated boots, which have evidently belonged to some bigger man than himself, drives the spare mules furiously hither and thither, to the barking of all the curs in the neighbourhood. The men have donned their best go-to-meeting clothes for the occasion, and swell about, clanking their spurs and showing their clean frilled shirts and gaudy sashes, with great complacency.

By the side of the waggons rides the capataz or overseer, directing the muleteers, with much unnecessary gesticulation and cracking of a long whip. The suburbs of San Antonio are not very extensive, and we soon emerge into the flat, brush-covered plains, and the mules, of which many are half broken, and some in for the first time, now steady down into a soberer pace, although one of them kicks himself free and escapes into the chaparral. After an exciting chase of about a mile and a half, he is lassoed, and brought back kicking vigorously, and we all feel much enlivened by the incident. On the first day it is customary to make a short stage, as nothing is as yet in good working order, and so we halt for the night on the banks of a small creek, the capataz having first ridden forward to ascertain if there is wood, grass, and water — the three requisites of a camping ground. We reach the camp, the waggons are formed into a square, the interstices between them being secured by hide ropes; the harness is taken off the mules with marvellous celerity, and placed neatly underneath the waggons. Round the inside of the square a portable manger, filled with Indian corn, is speedily erected, and the mules fall into line to eat. As it is the first night out, the grass bad, and the mules near home, we have brought hay for them, and they are not let out of the square all night. On other occasions it is general to let them pasture loose under a guard, the wildest being hobbled. The camp-fires are next lit, the Mexicans having all the dexterity of the Indian for lighting fire in all weathers; wind, rain, sleet, or damp wood, does not make a bit of difference — the fire is always lit, and that soon. Then coffee is boiled, beans put in a pan to stew, bacon fried, and the cook mixes a rough sort of bread, which is baked in covered iron pots, called by the Texan cowboy a skillet, made of maize flour. We enjoy our frugal supper, then we gather round the fire to smoke our cigarettes, and, as the evening is chilly and threatens a Norther, indulge in a stiff glass of hot toddy. Our sleeping arrangements are simple; rolled up in blankets we go to roost, some round the fire, others on the top of the bales of cotton with which the waggons are loaded, and some underneath; and as we are so near the town no watch is kept. Seven days of monotonous, uneventful travel through rolling prairies, and we reach the frontier town of El Paso del Aguila, on this side of the Río Grande. On the other bank, facing the American settlement, is the small Mexican town of Piedras Negras, having a pretty *plaza de armas* and a ruined church. The town is a den of contrabandists, thieving customhouse officers, and mongrel Americans, kept in order by a beggarly, bare-footed crew of soldiers, of which seven hundred, cavalry and infantry, are always in the barracks.

The Río Grande is the boundary between two countries as distinctly separate from each other in every respect as Western Europe is from Asia. From the wooden shanty of the American, in all its appalling ugliness, his tinned meats and his universal shoddy, we come upon a country where the schoolmaster is not yet abroad (excepting always in the capital itself), where the towns, with their flat-roofed houses and adobe jacals date mostly from the time of the old conquistadores; a country where the artist may luxuriate in almost perfect specimens of Hispano-Mauresque architecture, and the people, idle and thievish, are brown and picturesque and have all the Southern love for the *dolce far niente*,[2] and all the Southerner's materialism. They like lounging about in their plazas, dressed in wide white drawers, a sarape thrown carelessly over the shoulder, glowering suspiciously at the stranger, and gloomily calculating what amount of profit might possibly accrue from a quick stab of the knife dexterously driven home into that stranger's shoulder. All day they lie on the benches, enjoying, in a dull, sensual way, the scent of flowers and the dreaming invoked by lying in the sun watching a fountain splashing. A very small percentage of the people are shopkeepers; usually they are foreigners or of Spanish descent, although the trading spirit is universal, and the sharpest

Yankee would find it difficult to overreach a Mexican. Indeed the Mexican discovers a wonderful aptitude for petty trading, and is a hard man to beat at bargaining. It may, however, be set down as a general rule that he contents himself by demanding two-thirds more than the price he means to take eventually. Were you to give the sum he demands, at once, without chaffering or expostulation, he would feel intense disappointment at the negotiation not having been conducted on your part upon a more business-like and serious footing, but will slink away at last triumphant at having swindled "el pobre extranjero", for thus he designates you (with infinite contempt tempered by pity) when describing the progress of the negotiation to his admiring compatriots.

But to return to our waggons. The country outside Piedras Negras is wild and romantic, reminding one rather of some parts of Wales, and, as we go farther on, the flat waste plains, covered with short wiry grass and sage bush, slope gradually up to the horizon; a barrier of rocky and precipitous mountains shuts them in. On these wide desolate prairies range herds of deer and antelope, and we saw numbers of these animals who, raising their gracefully poised heads for an instant as they smelt danger, scudded away in the distance with all the velocity of the wind. Troops of wild turkeys defile across the road, and once or twice wild hogs with bristling crests and white tusks glare cautiously out from among the brushwood. Of bears and wolves there are plenty amongst the mountains. Little black pigs run squealing and grunting about every hut, hens and chickens peck about in the road, the dogs and cats lie sleeping in the sun, and even the miserable *pelón*, with its hairless body and hideous face, finds some happiness in life. The donkey is "tied around" munching its maize stalks placidly. The chapel, with its campaniles, in which swing too heavy bells, built of rough stones apparently just stuck one on the top of the other, and its carved wooden portal surmounted by fading frescoes, makes one feel as if one had suddenly been transported to the Middle Ages.

The rivers are few and far between, and on their banks, whenever practicable to coax the soil to bear a crop of Indian corn or of frijoles, is situated a cluster of miserable huts, or even a small town, inhabited by vaqueros, shepherds, and the nondescript slouching loungers to be met with all over Mexico. A few straggling streets of flat-topped houses, built of adobe, each standing by itself in a little garden or courtyard, overgrown with weeds and flowers growing amicably side by side, a plaza, a waste of brown sand, with some red plaster benches scattered around a few stunted trees, and you have a Mexican country-town. A dreamy air of torpor and listlessness hangs over the place which almost sends one to sleep. Everything is of a uniform brown, from the adobe huts to the leather clothes of the vaqueros and the burnt up patch of grass in the plaza. This monotony is never broken except by an alarm of Indians or the customary biennial revolution. A *tendajo*, the solitary store of the village, overlooks the plazuela, kept by a paunchy Mexican, who unites the functions of alcalde and shopkeeper — the great man of the place, and usually a rogue.

By the doorway outside hang strings of red pepper, garlic, onions, dried meat, and horse gear; and inside are sold saddles, sarapes, mescal, and cheap crockery, and goods of the worst class from the United States, retailed here at exorbitant prices. Tied beside the door, half a dozen lean mustangs stand patiently all day under a burning sun, buried under heavy saddles and ponderous stirrups, the saddle covered by an old sheepskin, a rusty rifle hanging on one side, and the redoutable lazo on the other. They will remain here till sundown, when their masters, stupified by mescal, saunter into the street apathetically smoking cigarettes, and ride home at full gallop, throwing their arms wildly about and shouting and laughing wildly.

The outskirts of these villages are all more or less dangerous. Although on the frontiers of Mexico there are no regular highway robbers, as in the interior of the country, yet, on the smallest suspicion that the unfortunate traveller carries money, several of the principal householders of the village would be sure to band together and follow him out. In fact, it may be said that the whole population are thieves, only kept in check by their own phlegmatic temperament; not a shadow of law existing. The few cultivated fields hedged with aloes, the sign of habitation, had long merged into the desolate plain when we meet a man on a donkey. He is taking an arrow, which he picked up early that morning, into the town to show the alcalde that Indians are about. Near the *charco*, where we stop to light a fire and have luncheon, a flock of scraggy goats and sheep are feeding, guarded, or rather accompanied, by a shepherd asleep under a bush. These shepherds lead a hard life. Sent out in charge of from two to three thousand sheep, they often pass three or four months away from their homes and families, out alone in the plains. About once a week they kill a sheep; sometimes, if short of clothes, fashioning the skin into a jacket; and occasionally a ragged urchin on a donkey brings some coffee and tobacco. At the sound of the waggon wheels crashing amongst the brushwood he looks up sleepily, but does not ask for news of any kind. We tell him that Indians are about, but even this fails to arouse him from his apathy. We ask him if he is not afraid that they will come upon him suddenly some day and kill him, alone as he is, without even a dog to give him warning. He answers that he has given a candle to San Rufino; and pointing to an ancient firearm, bell-mouthed and worm-eaten, and warranted at the least to miss fire five times out of ten, he observes, with a touch of vanity, "Y pues, señor, yo tengo mi rifle."[3] The poor fellow takes the cigarette we offer with a brightened eye, and is thankful for the dry beef and beans which the capataz hands to him. Suddenly his lean brown finger points far away to a cloud of dust in the mountains, and he remarks quite casually, "Los bárbaros con una caballada."[4]

Upon arriving at Juárez, we found that the savage Mescalero Apaches[5] had on the previous night murdered a family in the neighbourhood and burnt their hut. The mother was pierced through by a lance; and a boy, a rickety-looking little fellow about two years old, was found amongst the bushes, where he had crept for safety. His brothers and sisters to the number of ten were all killed. We talked over the dismal occurrence at night over the camp-fire, the coyotes howling dismally in the distance, as we sit round smoking cigarettes[6] and endeavouring to chew hunks of tough dried meat, before wrapping ourselves in blankets and going to sleep. We knew we were in wild and dangerous country, where there was a chance of Indians, and before turning in every rifle was put ready to hand, in case of alarm, and the animals carefully staked. Before morning there was a false alarm. The horses and mules were restless, and snorted every now and then, and as the first method of attack by Indians is to stampede the horses, an extra guard were roused up so as to be on the alert. Nothing else occurred, however, to give cause for apprehension. Long before daylight we had left our night's camping ground far behind, and at dawn are skirting the Sierra Madre, or main range of the Rocky Mountains, whilst on every side of us mountains rise upon mountains. It is a very beautiful sight which meets us as we rub our eyes and gaze drowsily out. But drowsiness soon passes away as we watch the delicate opaline lights playing on the faces of the cliffs, amber deepening into gold through every phase of hue, which again changes into a faint flush of rose colour, gradually deepening into the lightest, tenderest shades of purple. The sides of the mountains become like jewels where the light subtly plays amongst the shadows, whilst their base is lost in billowy clouds of dense white mist. Amongst these mountains lies a curious flat tableland, which, though it is not of great height, is of considerable extent, and surrounded on every side by precipitous crags. It is quite inaccessible; so much so that two or three men, if properly provisioned, might keep the place against an army as long as they chose, the only pass to the top having been blasted by gunpowder through the live rock, and closed at the bottom by strong iron gates. On the summit is an immense cattle establishment, where above ten thousand head of cattle find pasturage. They are driven up in the spring, and are brought down again to sell in the autumn when fat. This unique cattle farm, which is the property of an Irishman, one Mr. Patrick Milman, who, arriving in Mexico many years ago without a halfpenny, has made here a large fortune. It is about twenty miles on the Monterrey side from Lampazos, a town which forms the boundary between the plain and hill country.

Here, too, cut in the rocks, and on the walls of caves — of which there are many — many specimens of Comanche picture-writing can be found. We were told by the majordomo of the Hacienda de la Mesa, which also belongs to Mr. Milman, that by one of these caves, having communication with a subterranean passage, the Mescaleros are accustomed to come in when on the war trail.

We arrived at Villaldama — so named after one of the heroes of the Independence[7] — as the sun went down behind the deep dark purple of the mountains, and shed a last gleam upon the little river fringed with poplars and willows. Later on, after supper, we strolled into the picturesque little plaza, the moon glinting on the sharp and broken outline of the ruined monastery church, and falling full upon the middle of the plaza, making the black shadows cast by the houses deeper and more intense, with the bright lights and the dark shadows playing with and embracing one another, as it were; and the background of hills in sharp relief against the clear sky formed a picture of harmony and quiet, which many miles of fatiguing and dusty travel disposed us to enjoy to the full.

About forty miles on this side of Monterrey we come upon vast palm woods, which accompany us more or less the whole way on our road to Mexico.

We were very glad to see the Cerro de la Silla of Monterrey looming in the distance, and gladder still to find ourselves comfortably ensconced in the *Mesón del Comercio*, in a clean, cellar-like room, with grated windows and barred doors, looking on to a pretty patio planted with pomegranate trees with vivid scarlet flowers, and another tree, slim and graceful, which had come from Italy, with bunches of yellow flowers and large, palmated leaves. A Spanish well in the centre, and a large drinking fountain for horses, at which some interior men were watering their mules; these last fantastically decked out with headgear made of red worsted and set round with little bits of looking-glass. These men, and some rough, two-wheeled country carts in the corner of the courtyard, form a group of such inimitable picturesqueness that, tired and hungry as we are, I make my husband jump with impatience whilst I transfer it to my sketch-book.[8] We dine at a little booth in the Plaza de Comercio, on roast kid and chocolate. The women eye us suspiciously, and ask if we are *extranjeros*, and where we come from. When we tell her she remarks incredulously, "Caray! Está muy lejos,"[9] and goes back to her innumerable pipkins; for the cooking operations are carried on at one end of the little kitchen whilst we dine at the other.

These are very simple, one must confess; a hearth consisting of a large slab of stone raised four feet above the ground, and covered with all manner of funnily shaped vessels cooking on the charcoal embers, kept red hot by a small boy with a huge fan. A dead kid is hanging by the hearth, from which every now and then the good woman slices a bit to fill up her pots; whilst in front of us we have a good view of the slaughterhouse. This, however, we do not appreciate probably at its proper value, as with most of the customers, who saunter in to take their chocolate and goat's milk, this seems to be the favourite seat.

The cathedral here is not satisfactory to the eye, being modern and very ugly, plastered over, and painted a sort of blue tartan on a surface of yellow ochre, which is almost too grotesque to be entirely repulsive. However, the distressing ugliness of the cathedral is made up for by the old convent of San Francisco, which is in ruins, and overgrown by shrubs and weeds, and the Palacio del Obispo,[10] now dismantled and used as a barracks for artillery, most charmingly situated on the slope of a hill overlooking the orange gardens of Monterrey. This last is a very fine specimen of the earliest Spanish American architecture, with a dome-shaped roof, and was probably built at about the beginning of the seventeenth century. Monterrey is very beautifully situated in a valley amongst the mountains, over which domineers the remarkable Cerro de la Silla, with its furrowed sides, which is the exact shape of a Mexican saddle.

The valley of Monterrey is indeed a kind of paradise for fertility and abundance of water. The road is shaded on either side by enormous pine trees and bushy thickets of flowering shrubs, figs, aguacates, and orange trees, borne down with abundance of fruit, pomegranates covered with blossoms of brilliant red, through which the traveller catches charming glimpses of the interiors of the brown jacals, before the door of which sit pigs, fowls, dogs, and naked children, in a happy family, whilst the mother and women of the house wash their rags in the brook hard by.

A donkey is tied up in one corner, — a mild-eyed lovable, very patient creature, — a little colt eating at her side; whilst the thin horse of the owner is tethered to a tree, and a handful of straw scattered before him. We are not in the interior of Mexico until we have passed the Valley of Santa Catalina and the picturesque old town of Saltillo; indeed, the interior does not really commence until San Luis Potosí. The day after leaving Saltillo, we camped in an arid gorge amongst the mountains, covered with palms, where two Indians — sole survivors of forty Mescalero captives taken from Santa Rosa in waggons, and fastened to one another by chains, caged like wild animals, and shown as a curiosity to all the towns through which they passed, to be imprisoned at Chapultepec[11] — had murdered a Mexican and his wife travelling to Saltillo to get work. The Indian killed the wretched man by repeated stabbing with a blunt knife, whilst the female Indian strangled the wife with a bit of string. The Mexicans had two dogs. One followed in the cart in which the bodies were carried for burial, lying on his dead master's breast; and the other, refusing to be comforted, wandered restlessly up and down the road, refusing all consolation. All night they had lain by the bodies of the dead people, the faithful watchers over the sacredness of death. The place was wild beyond description as the light of day broke upon it. Far-away mountains covered with mist, beyond which lay the Indian country, a *país desconocido*,[12] desert and uninhabited save by the red man and the buffalo; whilst nearer one rugged mountains rose against the grey windy sky, and two lonely palms, emblems of the strange and weird solitariness, rose up like slim bodies with fantastic heads against the sky. We offered a reward for the dog, but the muleteers could not lasso him, as he was very shy and ran away at one's approach.

All the way to Mexico we came upon traces of these wretched Indians. One of them we saw hanging from a tree by the roadside, but his features were quite undistinguishable, and the body fearfully swollen by exposure to the sun. From one of the small towns past San Luis Potosí twenty soldiers, well-armed with rifles, were sent out after them. They came upon the Indians as they were lying asleep at midday. The two male Indians made a most gallant resistance, their only arms being the bows and arrows which they had constructed after their escape from Mexico. Heaven alone knows how or with what materials. They managed to cover the escape of the women, killed one soldier, and wounded many before they got away. One of the women was drowned in swimming a river, but her child was saved, and the padre of the village, who was present at the combat, and the only man who did not wholly lose his presence of mind on seeing the Indians, offered to take charge of it to bring it up. The other woman crept into the bushes and was saved. Some days after this, a vaquero observed two Indians in the mountains, the woman riding and the man running by her side; but of nine captive Indians who had escaped from the cages of Chalpultepec, it is probable that only two persons survived to relate the sad fate of their companions to their brothers of the tribe, thirty-one of the poor creatures having died from starvation and smallpox in captivity. The escape of these two was wonderful and heroic when one considers the insuperable dangers and most terrible privations they must have suffered whilst effecting it. Totally without arms, except those they were able to construct for themselves in those dreary mountains where there is no vegetation but prickly pear, and game scarcely exists; dependent for the barest subsistence upon the animals they might chance to capture or shoot; without water amongst country sandy and arid to a degree, except that collected in the crevices and hollows of the rocks after the dew had fallen; running barefoot over thorns and sharp flints; suffering from the very intense cold of winter nights, high up amongst the mountains, — it seems almost incredible to us that even their powers of endurance were equal to a journey, and such a journey, of twelve hundred miles! When we last heard of them in Saltillo, they were only about a hundred miles from their tribe, and I hope that they survived to tell the story of their feat to their friends, and to surfeit themselves, amid great rejoicing, with the meat of the buffalo.

After leaving Gómez Farías,[13] the country changes, and we pass once more through sandy plains covered with sage brush, and inhabited by the prairie dogs — shrewd little animals, who sit on their burrows and watch us pass, occasionally giving a small sharp yelp like that of a new-born pup. About four miles out of Gómez Farías we pass over a bare, windswept prairie, which the muleteer points out to us as the Llano de la Guerra, where the Mexicans, under the Cura Hidalgo, gained a signal victory over the Spaniards.[14] By the wayside we note numberless mounds covered with heaps of stones, a wooden cross stuck in the middle, or a square plaster niche containing crucifixes and faded chaplets of flowers. They are the graves of those "muertos por los indios y los ladrones."[15] There were fewer of the former than of the latter. Every traveller adds a stone to the heap as a tribute of respect to the dead lying beneath; for who knows what may be his own fate in this lawless country, where life and property are equally insecure. A larger heap of blackened stones and another cross is pointed out to us as "un pueblito, señor, quemado por los bárbaros."[16] It seems that the bárbaros had come down out of the mountains on to the lonely village, which they had burnt down, with all its wretched inhabitants. We camp for the night within the enceinte of a large hacienda. These haciendas are well worth a few words, as they form one of the most remarkable features in Mexican travel. They are a kind of oasis in the desert; and after miles of dusty travelling in a jogging waggon, it is pleasant to descry on the horizon its yellow walls, gleaming in the declining sunlight, surrounded by orange gardens and green fields, and the tower of an old church appearing in the distance. They were mostly built when the Spanish ranchero made of his house a kind of fortification to repel the attacks of Indians. You can see the loopholes which have been pierced in the solid walls for musketry, and the places where they used to mount small cannon. The courtyard is sometimes of immense extent, being often a quarter of a mile in diameter; in it are the owner's house, the majordomo's hut, a flour mill, a store where the bookkeeper pays the people employed on the hacienda in kind, a church, a mesón where travellers stop, exactly like an Eastern caravanseri, and the jacals of the labourers, who sometimes number above a hundred. The owner generally lives in Mexico or one of the large towns, and leaves the place under the management of a majordomo, who receives from one hundred to hundred and fifty dollars a month, only visiting the place occasionally to see that all is going on smoothly. In fact, Mexico is a kind of Ireland, on a larger scale.[17] The Mexican is generally a great party politician, and all those of opposite factions live by robbing one another as much as possible. In the revolutions, as all law ceases, bands of armed men, under the pretence of fighting for "las leyes, la constitución, libertad de conciencia y el hogar,"[18] wander about the country seeking whom they may devour. The rich ranchero rarely trusts himself for long upon his own estate. His country dwelling is generally very pleasant, and is built in the old Spanish style, round a courtyard full of blossoming fig-trees, roses, and fragrant shrubs, which shade, and nearly hide, the stone fountain in the middle. There are stone seats under the dark, cool portico, on which you may lie all day and watch the golden sun sleeping on the flags without. Stone steps go up to the top of the flat-roofed buildings, which were no doubt useful when the master was wont, in the times of the Indians, to sweep the plains with an anxious eye, ever on the alert for signs of danger.

The inside of his house is sparsely furnished, but the stone floors and heavy tables shine with cleanliness. Windows are unheard of, and all the light comes in at the open door. Furniture is scanty; the old worm-eaten chairs and tables dating from the conquistadores, in whose times the ponderous oak and stamped leather were probably new; but now these quaint dwelling-houses are too often furnished with cheap French goods from the city of Mexico, and the lumbering antiquities of their ancestors devoted to be cut up for fuel. An old man we met in one of the haciendas spoke regretfully of the Spaniards. Although hard task-masters, he said, property was safe; at least, there was only one master instead of many.

Near Matehuala, a town where the silver is brought from the mountains of Catorce to be smelted, the convoy taking the silver to the capital passes us. A heavy, old-fashioned coach bears the conductor, and after him come lumbering ambulances travelling with him for safety, and a heavy cart containing the chests of silver, guarded by sixty cavalry and some foot-soldiers, all small men, round-shouldered, but hard walkers, in dirty brown holland suits and bare feet, with or without sandals. A regiment on the march generally does fifty miles a day, the officers having full power to stick their swords through the laggers. The soldiers rarely eat meat, and they may consider themselves happy and well cared for if they get three plates of beans a day and half a dozen tortillas. Some only get one, and very little of that if the general in command happens to be stingy, and has no special object to gain by winning his men's affections. When they arrive at a well, after a day's march in the tropical sun and suffocating sand, a guard is placed, so that no soldier can drink until after a certain interval, and when the interdict is withdrawn they throw themselves down and lap like dogs. I heard of one officer allowing twenty men to drink at once, to give an example to the rest of the men, who had been complaining, and he left them behind him dying. My informant, the officer in question, said that they just went off like doves ("se empalomaron todos").[19]

We also meet the stage coach, which does the journey from Mexico to San Luis Potosí in four days. The most remarkable fact concerning it is that the poor passengers seem to be the legitimate prey of the banditti, who occasionally vary proceedings by attacking the conductor — the last time not quite so successfully as they at first imagined. They found that they could neither drag the iron chest, bearing their prize, away from the road amongst the bushes, nor could they force an opening anywhere. Fires were lighted round the chest, but without effect; and eventually the alcalde got hold of it almost uninjured. But I am sure, from my experience of Mexican character, that he endeavoured to open it himself before restoring it to the Government.

I should think in no town on the continent of America are to be found so many and such beautiful churches as in the far-named San Luis Potosí. Besides a magnificent cathedral built of yellow stone, and carved on every side with figures of saints and apostles, and the convent Church of San Agustín, with its rich tessellated dome of many coloured tiles, you may find in almost every out-of-the-way nook and corner a chapel, façade of a convent, or some old ruinous house, over the gates of which figure the armorial bearings of some proud family of Castile, the significance of which is lost to the Mexican of to-day. Since the Spaniards left Mexico, this town, once the richest in Spanish America, has dwindled down to forty or fifty thousand inhabitants. The most interesting sight to be seen in San Luis is the *alhóndiga*, filled always with men, women, and half-naked children, squatting round baskets of the strangest wares. Besides fruits and flowers, they are selling fried insides of aloes, and palm flowers cooked in oil, to suit Mexican palates. Donkeys stand meekly in the dusty alley, packed with fruit from the *tierra caliente* by the coast, or large vessels of Mexican pottery from Querétaro. *Fruteros* in wide white drawers block the way, bearing on their heads baskets of the delicious hot country fruits — mangoes, cocoanuts, chirimoyas, bananas, plátanos, pomegranates, oranges, sweet lemons, zapotes, both black and green, and shaddocks, piled one upon the other, and the whole surmounted by a bit of vivid colour in the shape of a bouquet of scarlet blossoms. The mesóns are invaded from morning to night by vendors. The first thing which salutes your ear as you wake are the hoarse, prolonged cries of the itinerant merchants. Then you have them upon you in full cry — woven shawls for women, sarapes, Birmingham and Liège swords mounted gaudily in ivory or brass, Mexican bits, made of wrought iron inlaid with silver, bundles of plaited horsehair reins, and saddle gear of all descriptions, pistols, *dulces*, and dried fish. All day long the cry is "Still they come." Buy from one, and the whole brotherhood will be upon you shortly, by their fifties, and will not cease to pester you until you have shaken the dust of San Luis Potosí from off your feet. As we were lounging in the plaza facing the cathedral, idling the time away by sitting in the sun and smelling the violets which grow in all Mexican plazas, a beggar approached begging, "Un claco, señor, un mero claco, por todos los santos y la madre de Jesucristo."[20] We threw the poor creature a *medio*, and placidly listened as he bestowed on us his benediction. At last he shuffled off. In a short time an old woman with a palsied hand, led by a child, came past, and she stopped short before us. This time we were more obdurate, and our obduracy and impatience increased as we saw ourselves the centre of a group of mendicants, all in various stages of abject misery and deformity. The maimed, the halt, and the palsied surrounded us. We fairly turned tail and fled; but to our horror and disgust, on looking round, we discovered the whole lot after us at full speed — such a race of the maimed, palsied, the halt and the blind, I never saw even at Naples or Granada. We hurried into the mesón and locked our door; they regularly sat down and besieged us. The sketch-book did us service in ridding us of some of these dreadful people, and made us objects of dread and aversion, especially as they conceived us the possessors of the evil eye.

At four o'clock it is the custom of the better classes to promenade in the alameda, a burnt-up garden in the suburbs. The regimental band plays at the barrack gates, and caballeros, in enormous white hats laden with silver, and short jackets, prance their horses round the square. The ladies make some attempt at European garments, but it is much to be wished that they would stick to the mantilla, thrown loosely round the shoulders.

Again the country changes as we leave San Luis Potosí on the hot dusty road to Mexico. The dust flies up in clouds, and muleteers and waggons lose their natural colour and become dingy white. We can scarcely breathe for the fine dust, which penetrates to the lungs. It is so penetrating that the train men on the San Luis Potosí road to Mexico rarely if ever live long, and nearly all die of consumption. On either side of us we see nothing but scorched plains, covered with many different kinds of cactus and thorny brushwood. Dim blue mountains rise in the distance, but the cactus is certainly the chief feature in the landscape. Hedges of palm and cactus enclose huge flat fields of tall magueyes (the species of aloe from which the Mexican drink, mescal, is made, and the finer quality, tequila), and this is the only vegetation that there is between San Luis and the capital. However, the cactus in flower is pretty, and one wonders that such prickly, ungrateful things can bear such lovely flowers, which are something like the hedgerow rose in form, but of every shade of colour, shading from the deepest scarlet to the faintest tinge of pink, and from gorgeous orange to pale lemon yellow. Others are white or variegated. We are continually passing large haciendas, and we hail the clump of trees and the green alfalfa patches with delight. The maguey plants are worth a dollar apiece, and serve two purposes. By one process are made mescal and tequila (a better kind of mescal), and by the other, pulque, a turbid, whitish liquor, holding the same place with the Mexicans as beer does with us. The water is very bad here, alkaline, and injurious both to men and animals. The traffic on this road begins to get enormous. We meet trains of donkeys; their barefooted drivers, running beside them, are loaded with pottery and articles of the country; troops of Aztecs, lithe and agile, each carrying on his back about eighty or ninety pounds weight of large pots and vessels of baked clay. Their gait is a slow, swinging trot, and as they run they plait straw, holding the straw between the teeth and plaiting nimbly with the fingers. These men travel between San Luis Potosí and other towns of the interior, to the capital, and do about forty or fifty miles a day.

We sometimes breakfast at Indian huts by the wayside; as the women here, owing to the great traffic, make a living by cooking for the passers-by. They sell a stew of turkey, a kind of sweet porridge (atole), tortillas, and the universal black beans and coffee. They speak Spanish well, but Aztec better, and all their intercourse amongst themselves is carried on in the ancient language of the Children of the Sun.

In the city of Mexico the Aztec women make a hard livelihood by carrying jars of water to sell at the houses and bearing heavy burdens of all kinds, for which they have the strength of a horse. Under the heaviest load you never see a pure Indian walk, they always run, a blue blanket with a deep white border wrapped loosely round the body for a petticoat, and another fastened over the shoulders, and a head-dress, also of blue blanket, not unlike those worn by the Italian peasant women.

A Mexican town in the interior is highly curious and picturesque. There is generally an old church, with a bell-tower, in which hang massive iron bells forged long ago in Spain. Gateways, surmounted by coats of arms of the old Spaniards who once dwelt there, with cumbrous doors, studded with iron nails, take you back from the present to the past. Should they be open, you are lost in a wealth of colour, of flowers, and marble fountains and balconies, whilst the plazas are filled with orange and almond trees, and violets, and you may sit there all day listening to music.

Occasionally will pass a blind beggar, led by a little boy, and invoke on you all the blessings of God, "y de todos los santos,"[21] whilst another twangs a guitar. The notes are wild and plaintive, in the minor key, and a group of loiterers, moved by one spirit, strike up, in a peculiar nasal voice, a triste. Any of my readers who may have chanced to hear a blind beggar in Spain, will know how impossible it is to describe that low nasal singing given in unison. A *dulcero* comes by, and stays to listen, his arms swinging loosely by his side, as he cleverly balances a basket of sweetmeats, which rests upon a cushion on his head. Every one basks in the hot bright sun.

As it gets cooler, the bells clang out mournfully from many churches, and you stroll back through the old-fashioned streets, shaded by the tender green and beautiful blossoms of the trees, which are planted before every house, and wander back into the mesón, which is all bustle and confusion. A colonnade runs all round the patio, and underneath it open the doors of the travellers' rooms, which are not inviting, although they have one good property, that of being nearly as cool on a hot summer's day as an underground cellar — which for all the world they resemble. A stone bench runs out parallel with one of the walls, where you sleep; a mattress you are expected to provide yourself with on a journey, as there is probably not a spare one to be got in the mesón for love or money; sometimes, but not always, you are provided with a chair and a table, on which is placed a bottle with a rushlight in its neck. A boy brings you round a basin and a towel, which he waits for until you have finished with them, as he dare not leave them for fear of the traveller running off with them. With a sense of discomfort you stroll out again to have a look at the waggons. Passing through ponderous gates, you find yourself in the vast corral, two miles in circumference, with a well in the centre. The muleros are shouting and cursing, as they put their mules into rank to rub them down. It is surprising how the animals get to know the order which they are obliged to take, but the slow-witted mule gets an admonitory kick from the driver, and mules are very cunning. Fires are lit hither and thither about the yard, on which the muleros' beans are cooking, for the nights are cold for people who have only a thin sarape and linen drawers.

A tinkle of mule bells, and another waggon-train comes in, followed by a man with a herd of a hundred horses, which he is taking to sell in Mexico. Then come a troop of packed donkeys, driven by Indians in leather trousers — they are quickly unpacked and rastrojo brought.

In the morning we are off again, leaving the mesón by the red glare of torches.

We sleep in Jerez, and admire the old fortified house, or rather castle, of the old Spanish noble, the bodies of some of whose ancestors rest in the churchyard, built by the Conde de Jerez, a conquistador. At Huehuetoca we arrive thoroughly tired out with the long and dusty journey, and as we take our tickets at the station for Mexico, we are pleased to have arrived at our destination without the train having been robbed en route — an occurrence always likely to happen in Mexico. Mexico strikes us as being a large, handsome, somewhat French-looking town, and when we find ourselves in a comfortable French hotel, luxuriously supping on *côtelettes à la milanaise*,[22] and a bottle of burgundy, we are thoroughly able to appreciate the comforts of civilisation.

NOTES

1. From *The Christ of Toro* (London: Eveleigh Nash, 1908).
2. Sweet idleness.
3. "And, anyway, señor, I also have my rifle."

4. "The barbarians with a team of horses."
5. Graham will take up this theme of the Mescalero Indians and develop it in "A Hegira."
6. In fact, it was Gabrielle's excessive smoking that contributed to her premature death in 1906 at the age of forty-five.
7. As often happens, the place still survives, although the "hero" is long forgotten.
8. Gabriela was, in fact a competent artist. Apart from teaching drawing and painting in both New Orleans and Mexico, she has left some samples of her work which are to be found amongst the Graham papers at Harden.
9. "Good Heavens! That's awfully far away."
10. The Bishop's Palace.
11. See Graham's sketch "A Hegira" for more details of this incident.
12. "Unknown country."
13. Named after Valentin Gómez Farías, an able Liberal vice-president (1833-4) during the dictatorship of Santa Ana in Mexico in the post-Independence decades of the nineteenth century. After trying to initiate reforms and govern efficiently, he was forced to resign and go into exile in New Orleans.
14. The Plain of War, site of one of the battles won by Father Miguel de Hidalgo y Castillo, parish priest of the village of Dolores, whose famous Grito de Dolores (15 September 1810) became the cry of independence from the Spaniards. It is still celebrated as Independence day in Mexico.
15. "Killed by Indians and robbers."
16. "A village, señor, burned by the barbarians."
17. Both Gabrielle and Robert were concerned about the treatment of Ireland by the British. In fact, even as a Liberal M.P., Graham opposed Gladstone, his party leader and prime minister, on the Irish Question and Home Rule. In 1887 he was imprisoned for his protest against the jailing of Irish M.P. William O'Brien. See my article, "Don Roberto and Bloody Sunday," *Irish News*, 7 September 1965, p. 4.
18. "The laws, the constitution, liberty of conscience and family life." Unfortunately, even after the overthrow of Porfirio Díaz's dictatorship, the same crimes were being perpetuated in the name of the Mexican Revolution. Some would claim that there are still flagrant abuses today, in the face of an institutionalised revolutionary government.
19. See "A Chihuahueño" for a repetition of the same story by Robert.
20. "A penny, señor, just a penny, for the sake of all the saints and the mother of Jesus Christ."
21. "And of all the saints."
22. Chops done Milanese style.

EDITOR'S PREFACE

Since Gabriela's description is only of the waggon-train, it stops, of course, with the Grahams' arrival in Mexico City. Graham's sketch, "A Hegira," as we shall see, takes up the story more or less as they depart from Mexico again. Although he has not written in detail in his sketches about his life in Mexico, nor are there any letters from Mexico City, Graham displayed a great interest in Mexican affairs, politics, history, literature, etc., as his letters from Texas indicate. On his return to Britain, he maintained his interest in Mexico, corresponding with friends and writing letters to the press and book reviews in the British periodicals (see my Introduction, p. 1).

This sketch "Progress" was born out of the reading of a Mexican novel which had been sent to him. Graham, of course, was much more interested in the human qualities of the novel he describes, but he cannot avoid commenting on the political situation that precipitates the tragedy. The era that he describes, and that he was to return to in his letters and reviews, was the dictatorship of Porfirio Díaz (1876-1911), the half-lettered mestizo who surrounded himself with *científicos* or technocrats, and with the aid of foreign investment, especially from Britain and the United States, the social sciences, and the disciples of positivism and utilitarianism, hoped to drag Mexico into the twentieth century. This "progress" was not to be to the benefit of the poor and the Indians who were, however, to have the last word, come the revolution of 1910, which demanded "land and liberty," and the promise of agrarian and social reform.

The inhabitants of the village of this story, beyond the pale of progress and civilisation, resisted the dictator's attempts to extract taxes — the harsh consequences constitute the stuff of this powerful novel of Heriberto Frías. One is struck by the description of the isolated village, like so many in Mexico. One remembers Comala, as described by Juan Rulfo in *Pedro Páramo* (1955), and the hermetic village of *Al filo del agua* (1947), as depicted by Agustín Yáñez. The irony is, of course, that even *after* the Revolution such isolated villages still do not enjoy the benefits of the Promised Land in post-Díaz Mexico.

It is interesting that Graham should have been so struck by a novel, written at this time (1893-95), as to devote a whole sketch to it, and such a long one. Not long afterwards in Brazil, another novel was about to be written on exactly the same theme — resistance of villagers because of unjust taxation, government attempts to quell the rebellion, all set against the background of religious fanaticism. What is significant for Graham in both books, Heriberto Frías' *Tomochic* and the Brazilian novel *Os sertões* (1902) by Euclides da Cunha (translated into English by Samuel Putnam as *Rebellion in the Backlands* [Chicago: University of Chicago Press, 1944]), is the culmination of the political event in a manifestation of religious fanaticism, indicative of the strong messianic tradition that exists in Latin America.[1] Several decades later Graham was to take the Brazilian episode and the conduct of its protagonist Antonio Conselheiro, another religious fanatic, as the basis of his *A Brazilian Mystic* (1920).[2]

Although Heriberto Frías is not regarded as a first class writer,[3] *Tomochic* is interesting in that it prefigures not only the traditional *novela de la Revolución Mexicana* (like Azuela's *Los de abajo* [1916] and Martín Luis Guzmán's *El aguila y la serpiente* [1928]), but also the contemporary novel of the revolution, like the aforementioned works of Rulfo and Yáñez, and those of Carlos Fuentes — for example, the protagonist's adventures with his youthful symbolic peasant girl in the early episodes of *La muerte de Artemio Cruz*. More important, of course, is Graham's attitude to Frías' novel, and how it was to influence his view of Díaz, the Revolution, and the future of Mexico. More significant still is the human reaction, and how it was to be rendered in lasting artistic terms by Graham in this sketch and in future works like *A Brazilian Mystic*.

NOTES

1. For a comparable North American example of this phenomenon, one can cite the Jonestown tragedy, which took place, significantly, in Guyana.
2. It is interesting that Vargas Llosa has taken this same incident as the basis of his most recent novel, *La guerra del fin del mundo* (Barcelona: Plaza & Janés, 1981).
3. He may become a little better known with the publication of *Heriberto Frías* (Boston: Twayne, 1978) by James W. Brown in the World Authors series whose express function is to make foreign authors available to English-speaking readers.

PROGRESS[1]

A friend in Mexico sent me the other day a little book.[2]

The author, Heriberto Frías,[3] was quite unknown to me, but has become a friend.

It is asserted that some have been the hosts of angels unawares, a proposition most difficult of proof (or of disproof), for angels, in the self-same way as ghosts, are seen with the interior eye. But the book lies before me, in all the poverty of its cheap paper, and the faint, eye-searing print, which Spain apparently has left among its legacies to the republics which once were "jewels in her crown."

Printed in Mexico (Mancier Brothers, Iº del Relox), it has upon its outside cover a vignette of a little village in the Sierra Madre, known as Tomochic. A river runs in front, slow flowing, and its margin set about with tamarisks. It further is adorned with the presentment of a soldier of the republic that Porfirio Díaz rules; a rifle in his hand, his bandolier crossing his chest, his chin-strap stuck beneath his nose, and on his face, an air of "Mexico expects each man to look his best."

On a small scroll there is a vignette of a poblana girl, wearing her hair in the old Spanish fashion in a long thick plait, and with a cross and a rosary, sinister, sable, displayed upon a ground of rather sickly gules. But the keynote is given on the left corner of the page where a strange figure sits. Dressed all in grey, with deerskin sandals on his feet, kept on by straps which, like the garterings of Malvolio,[4] or those worn by a pifararo,[5] rise to his knee, with his hands crossed upon his Winchester, two bandoliers upon his chest, and one about his waist fastened by a long silver cross, he sits and looks out on the world, with all the realism that a bad portrait sometimes has in a supreme degree. His bushy beard and thick moustache, long and dishevelled hair, and hat thrown back almost to form an aureole, show the religious monomaniac or enthusiast (for all the difference in the term is but the exit of the enterprise), at the first glance.

A curious cloak, which rises almost to his ears in two peaked wings, completes the picture, which may, for all that I know, have been taken from the life. Upon the other outside covering of the work are some perfunctory advertisements of books, most of them translations from the French, setting forth the *Vida de Jesús*, by E. Renan, *Mi madre*, by one Hugo Conway, and lastly, *La Señorita Giraud mi Mujer*, by Adolphe Belot.[6]

These, with some works by Chateaubriand and Daudet, together with the beautiful *María*, especially described as a *novela americana* by Jorge Isaacs,[7] pretty well make up the list — a list which, for its catholicity of taste, does honour to the house that issues it.

Thus with prolixity I have set forth the outside of my little book sent from Tenochtitlán,[8] as when it came to me it did not strike me that I should be much moved by its contents.

Nobody knows or cares in what part of the world is situated the state and town known as Chihuahua.

Somewhere in South America would be the general answer to the question, and so it is not to be thought that the heroic struggle and the destruction of the remote and quite unfriended village of Tomochic should excite even a passing qualm, for we are worshippers of the accomplished fact.

But still it sometimes rises in my mind, what profits it although a man, in the attempt to gain his soul, should be successful and should lose the world, if the same soul when gained should prove to be so shrivelled and so hide-bound that it were better to have lost it gallantly and kept humanity intact?

Who with a spark of kindliness or feeling for humanity, having hit in his travels on some island lost in an undiscovered archipelago, on which the inhabitants lived in their own way, even although they had not heard of hell, but would not make it his first duty to forget its latitude and banish all remembrance of its longitude out of his head? Only by doing so could he fend off the servitude of taxes and of creeds from the poor islanders, the introduction of corruption, gin, and syphilis, and all the thousand woes that islanders endure from the misguided zeal of honest missionaries. Who does not feel as if a slug was crawling on his soul on reading in some missionary report of all their misdirected labours and their sufferings, and of the perils that they have endured, to turn some fine free race of savages, interesting to us by their customs and their relation to ourselves, into bad copies of our lowest class, waddling about in ill-made clothes and claiming kindred with us as brother "Klistians" in the Lord?

Our author paints the village for us with some art, and tells, half-sympathisingly, how the full misery of progress and of modern life passed over it, as avalanches fall upon a hamlet in the hills, destroying church and houses, men, women, children, cattle, and the crops, and leaving nothing living in their track.

The wicked villagers believed in God and in His power, and in especial held in esteem the works of Santa Teresa, her of Avila.[9] Their favourite exclamation was, "Long live the power of God!" which they preferred to "Damn me!" or to any of the forms of phallic exclamation which their countrymen had ever in their mouths.

But though the President, Porfirio Díaz, he whom the travelling globe-trotter beslavers with his praise for having rooted out the highway robbers and enthroned the sweaters in their place, did not much care about the pious objurgations of the Tomoches, one article of their belief was sure to cut him to the quick. Taxes, they held, were only due to God, and thus at the first step they placed themselves outside the pale of Christianity. This was the way the matter seemed to strike "Don Porfi," the imperial President.

The book begins with the impressions of a young officer who had been sent to join his regiment in the advance against the ruffians who had withheld their taxes, and passed their time in glorifying Santa Teresa and their God. We meet the callow officer, Miguel Mercado, in one of those rustic restaurants which form a feature of the life of northern Mexico, after a long march.

Smoking tamales and leathery tortillas, roast kid and turkey cooked with red peppers in a savoury stew, with dishes of black beans cooked in bacon fat, comprised the fare. The wine was that of Parras, mescal made from maguey, and its superior variety tequila, were the stronger drinks.

Here he finds all the officers of the regiment he has to join engaged at lunch. He learns that in the interior of the Sierra Madre a town composed of madmen had "pronounced."

To his astonishment, his comrades tell him that the forces of the Government have been twice driven back with heavy loss, and that a number of their officers and a lieutenant-colonel had been take prisoners.

No one can tell him why the little sierra-built town has set itself like Athanasius against the world.[10]

Still, all the people of Chihuahua were loud in admiration of the valour of the villagers and of their skill in arms. They showed a mute antipathy for the soldiers and against the central government. All that the Chihuahueños knew about Tomochic was that their chief was called Cruz Chaves, and that he preached a strange religion full of mysticism and a sanctity of life unknown to clergymen, mixed with wild ideas of communism unfit for the conversing of good business men.[11]

Orders to march, however, came at once, and the troops, with a quick-firing gun, struck into the vast arid prairies which stretch right from the Río Grande to the foothills of the great mountain range which runs all through the state. As they advanced across the steppe, its scanty vegetation white with alkali, in the far distance antelopes scudded away down wind, pillars of dust arose, and overhead vultures and eagles soared, whilst now and then the soldiers plodded through villages of prairie-dogs, who, seated on their mounds, looked at the approaching force, and as they neared their towns squeaked and rushed down into their holes, whilst the grave little owls, their fellow-dwellers in the waste, after a widening flight, alighted on the hillocks and blinked their eyes at the unusual sight.[12] The icy wind whistling down from the hills chilled to the bone, and as they passed a few lone ranches, it was seen that all the sympathy of the inhabitants was dead against the troops.

Beside the soldiers walked their women and their wives, shod with huaraches, having on their backs their cooking-pots. As they marched before the troops they looked (says Heriberto Frías) like some tribe of cannibals upon the march. Throughout the day the officers, as is the custom in the high plains of Mexico, did all they could to stop the soldiers drinking at the wells, knowing that drinking heated, at such altitudes, is almost certain death; but now and then the women, running up behind, contrived to slip a gourd of water into their hands, which they drank as they walked, in spite of every risk. And as they marched the women told them stories of the strange place that they were to attack, gleaned from the ranches that they passed upon the way.

Santa Teresa, it appeared, had blessed the rifles of her worshippers[13] so that each shot would have a victim, and no bullet fired, fall useless to the ground.

At last the column reached Guerrero and camped upon the alameda of the town, the peaks of the far mountains of the Sierra Madre showing sharp and blue, and seeming only a league or two away.

When the young officer Miguel Mercado had got some supper and began to talk with his companions of the day, news came that the lieutenant-colonel who had been taken prisoner by the men of Tomochic had been set free without conditions, and had rejoined their force. This naturally astonished every one, and when it then leaked out that the whole body of the fighting men of Tomochic reached to a hundred, and that each man, given his knowledge of the country and his skill in arms, was worth three soldiers, Miguel observed that it appeared as if a breath of icy wind had passed across the faces of his friends.

During his supper Mercado had observed a pretty girl who came into the rustic restaurant which, in a tent, is ready every evening in the frontier towns. As often happens when a man is just about to risk his life, his every sense was strung to breaking point. The image of the girl possessed him, and as he wandered up and down in the acute and bitter cold, he passed a cottage where he thought he would go in and ask if they had any drink to sell.

Just as he passed the threshold he heard a voice calling for coffee, with an oath. He went in, and on a rough camp-bed made of strips of ox-hide nailed to a wooden frame, from out a bundle of sarapes, he saw a head appear. It was that of a man of middle age, the hair was long and turning grey, the nose hooked, and the eyes piercing and red with drink.

Before him stood a girl half-dressed, with eyes cast down and trembling, and in an instant Mercado saw that she was the same girl who had occupied his thoughts. As he gazed at her the man called, "Julia, hurry up and bring my boots." The young man looked at her and saw that she was pretty and about fifteen. What was his horror and disgust, when the rough, long-haired giant had got up, to see her turning down the bed to find her handkerchief, and to remark that on the mattress she had left the impress of her body on the side next the wall.

He looked at her, and though (as Heriberto Frías says, with the simplicity and directness of the Spanish race) he was not handsome, yet he was young, and as his eyes met Julia's she turned red. Pointing towards a woman making tortillas just outside the door, Mercado said, "Is that your mother?" "No, my step-mother," the girl replied. "Ah, I thought she was your mother," said

Mercado. "And this ogre of a man?" "My uncle — but he is also — that is to say, we are not married, for the woman is his wife." Then she would say no more, and to Mercado's question of why she did not leave her husband-uncle, answered, "It is my father's wish. He is a saint, but does not know his brother. Santa Teresa sanctified him, and though they shot him, he rose from the dead, just as did Christ." "But you, who are you?" "I am the daughter of José Carranza, and I come from Tomochic."

Here Heriberto Frías breaks off into a description of Tomochic and of the causes which led to the revolt, which might as well have been at the commencement of the book. But who shall quarrel with an author, unless it be a critic (and there are few of them in the Sierra Madre), as to the method which he uses to let us know what he is going to impart. We take it all on trust, as we do sermons, rain, and Acts of Parliament. Reading all that he writes, one cannot but believe that the Tomochitecos must have all been mad.

It appears that Tomochic had been a frontier town always in warfare with the Apaches, and that once the immediate danger over, the inhabitants had settled down to the enjoyment of a kind of peace with arms. All carried guns, and used them frequently. All were religious, and in the parish church for many generations all the chief notables had been interred.

One sees the place dazzling with whitewash in the clear blue sky, or brown with sun-dried bricks, but as to this our author gives no details, so I will make it white.

The little sandy streets crossed one another at right angles, and emerged upon the plaza, where was built the church. All round the square stood seats of stucco painted in yellow ochre or in blue. Above them waved some straggling China trees, or ashes of Japan. The windows all had gratings of wrought iron; the doors were solid, and were studded thick with nails. Outside the actual town extended maize fields set with jacals in which the cultivators lived. The church was built of brick, daubed over white with stucco, and no doubt had been the chapel of some Franciscan mission, so many of which are to be seen upon the frontiers both of Texas and of Mexico. Horses stood blinking saddled all the day at every door and men wrapped in sarapes lounged so constantly against the sides of every house that all the angles of the walls were polished, and it seemed that the houses certainly would fall if the hard-working loungers were to move suddenly away.

There may have been some little shops in which some fly-blown wares were kept, with boxes of sardines, some macaroni, raisins of the sun, and bottles of mescal, tequila, whisky of the Americanos, boots, girths, cigarettes, and general stores, called *abarrotes* by the Mexicans, although the real meaning of the word is "dunnage", and signifies the packing used for the cargo of a ship. And yet an air of melancholy hung all about the place: an air of melancholy, but mingled with distrust, so that, when men heard noises in the night, their hands grasped pistol-butts laid ready to their beds; and in the daytime hearing anything unusual, they stopped their conversation with their eyes and ears strained open, as a coyote or a mustang listens when a twig crackles or a distant neigh is borne along the wind.

Lost in the mountains, far from roads, distrustful and distrusted, with its taxes dwindling and its offertory almost illusory, what wonder that Tomochic was neglected both by the Church and State?

But suddenly a wave of wild religion, which not infrequently breaks out in desert places, as at Mecca, or in Oman where El Wahab essayed the last Mahommedan reform,[14] swept on Tomochic and made it known, at least in Mexico.

The Governor of Chihuahua, one Carillo, having passed by the place, admired the pictures in the church and wished to take them to the capital. The inhabitants, who probably had never given them a thought before, rose as one man in their defence, and from that time the Governor and all the satellites of the dread majesty of law became anathema to the religious townsfolk in the hills. Usually all revolts arise from insufficient causes; the people bearing real evils as patiently as mules bear loads, or donkeys riders upon Hampstead Heath.

A girl from Tomochic having fallen in love with a good-looking minion of the law was left despairing, with a young solicitor, to face the world. The people, who no doubt were not more strict in matters sexual than ordinary hypocrisy demands, found themselves outraged, and at the moment that the times required, a man from God appeared.

His name was Don José Carranza — the Don no doubt mere courtesy, as is the case throughout America, where, as they say, "the treatment is general in our republics."

News came that on a day he would arrive and set to work to prove his thaumaturgic skill. He came, and proved to be an old and feeble man, but with him brought a wife a great deal younger than himself. He also brought a brother, one Bernardo, who had long left the village, having been expelled for theft.

But now he came triumphant and half-drunk, carrying a rifle in his hand, and giving out that he was now a soldier under Jesus Christ, and quite regenerate.

Saints, as it often happens with rude peoples, seem to be chosen for their lack of wit. This does not mar their saintship, for there is usually to hand some man, either fanatical or scheming, to take them under his protection and stand between them and the world.

This was the case in Tomochic, for there lived there a family called Chaves, Indian fighters to a man, withal religious, straight shooters, charitable, honest, and much respected in the town. The oldest was called Cruz, and he appears to have been a natural leader, and a man illuminated, as Mahommed was — a preacher and a rifle shot, some forty years of age, tall, dark, and with the steady eyes which show a spirit obstinate and bold.

After the "saint" had made his entrance with his edifying brother and his train of devotees, the vicar, who seems to have had some few remains of common sense, preached to the people, and exhorted them to turn away from folly, when suddenly Cruz Chaves rose in the body of the church, and, walking to the pulpit, thus addressed the priest:—

"In the name of the great power of God, I, His poor policeman, tell you to withdraw."

The priest, alone and unsupported, naturally withdrew.

Then, so to speak, was the abomination of desolation set up on the altar, and Saint José Carranza reigned supreme.

But he did more than this, for some one having told him that he was really Saint Joseph risen from the dead, he got into his head that in all things he must assimilate his conduct to that his prototype pursued. So calling up his brother Bernardo, the convicted thief, he gave him all his property, and, not content with that, his wife, although this second gift may perhaps have been not so great a sacrifice as at first sight it would appear. His daughter Julia he had intended for a holy virgin, who should work miracles and cast out Lucifer, but she, too, he gave to the convicted thief. Then, either pushed by madness or religious zeal, or set on by his brother, he held, as it were, a family council, and informed his people that he was tired of being but a saint, and now intended to be God.

So far the movement would appear to have been the work of idiots and of rogues, but underneath them lay a real fund of true fanaticism.

The Chaves family, which seems to have been composed of honest but pig-headed mystics, took the reins, and soon Tomochic grew to be respected as a place where men, although they paid no taxes, practised a sort of rough and ready justice, and recognised no other power than God's, for the poor "saint" soon fell into a state of stupid drunkenness.

But as the world which, though it commonly affects to obey God's laws, can never bear to see its theories really put in practice, soon began to kick. The Government in Mexico, which could not understand God's laws without man's taxes, promptly endeavoured to reduce the erring villagers by force of arms. The first attempt proved unsuccessful, and an enormous booty fell into the hands of Chaves, who acted as God's general in the fight. The people of Tomochic grew to be known as honourable men throughout Chihuahua, and the trains of mules with silver coming from the mines passed all unguarded near the village, knowing that not a man would try to stop them on the way.

The schism grew, and soon showed signs of spreading through the state, until the Govenment was forced to take the matter up for its own credit, and sent the expedition in which Mercado found himself, and which was now upon the march.

Bernardo and his two wives had been sent off by Chaves, who feared his bad example on the people of Tomochic, to spy upon the enemy at Guerrero, the younger woman passing as his daughter, to avoid scandal amongst the weaker brethren who had not chosen to accept the prophet of the sierra as a god.

Between him and Mercado a curious friendship rose, half brought about through the attraction which repulsive men and things occasionally exercise, and partly because it gave Mercado opportunities of seeing and of talking to the girl.

Little by little the inevitable occurred.

At first the gentle language and kind manners of the young officer attracted her, until at last one day he kissed her suddenly, and then (it is not I but Heriberto Frías who philosophises) there awoke in her the natural sensuality of youth, which the brutality of her tyrant had banished utterly.

Soon came the order for the column to advance, and after a wild meeting of the younger officers to celebrate the march, Mercado sallied out at night, wrapped in his cloak, to bid farewell to Julia before he set out for the fight.

These same good-byes are always perilous; but yet who would forgo them with all they mean and lead to, for human nature loves to reason out the dangers of a thing and then confront them, and when the worst has come, console itself with saying that the flesh is weak.

Miguel and Julia did not make the exception which is said to prove the rule, although of all the follies which mankind has crystallised in speech, surely this aphorism bears the palm. He went, as Holy Scripture says the adulterer goes, by night, wrapped in the cloak of darkness, saying no man will see, found the door shut, and knocking, it was opened by Julia in her shift, thinking that he who knocked was Don Bernardo, who in fact had remained drinking in the town.

There is a Scottish story of a doctor of old days who having bought a mare essayed to ride her, and what happened was related by his servant, thus: "The first kick landed the puir doctor on the pommel, the next between the mare's lugs; from thence his subsequent transition to the ground did not tak' long."

When about midnight Mercado left the rancho, conscious that he had perhaps but added to the miseries of Julia's life, he recollected that the column marched at daybreak, and, wrapping himself in his cloak, lay down beneath a tree upon the outskirts of the town, to sleep. The bugle woke him, as it seemed, almost before he had well closed his eyes. Struggling already dressed upon his feet, he ran to place himself upon the right flank of his company. As usually occurs in all campaigns, the column did not march at the time ordered, and Miguel had time to think upon his brief possession of the girl.

He saw her trembling and ashamed, loving and yet afraid to give herself to him because of her disgrace, himself imploring and Julia resisting, and then his taking her almost by force amidst her tears.

Vaguely he recalled that she had told him all her story, and that her monstrous husband was a spy sent by the people of Tomochic to tell them what was passing at the camp. He felt himself a traitor, both to his country and the girl, and drawn insensibly to see her once again on some pretext, stepped off to the jacal. He found it empty, with nothing left of its inhabitants but a lame donkey, which silently stood in the corral alone, its head hanging down sadly almost to the ground.

Then came the preparations for the march, and once again the column struck into the steppe.

Little by little from Guerrero the road ascends towards the enormous bulk of the backbone of Mexico. One seems to march for ever, and still the Sierra Madre looks as far away as at the beginning of the day. The thick white dust lies thick upon the dwarf mezquite and huisache trees, and makes the scattered cactuses loom like gaunt spectres on the plain.

Most of the streams are salt; the pasture salitrose,[15] and over all the sun glares down as it were made of brass. Nightfall just caught the column, which numbered over five hundred men and a quick-firing gun, at La Generala, a point at which the road begins to pass through pine woods and gigantic blocks of stone.

The soldiers, who had brought provisions from the town, were still in spirits, and the dull feeling which invades tired troops, making them fall at once to sleep, not even cooking food unless obliged, had not come over them. With songs and conversation round the fires they passed away the evening, and daylight found them once more on the road. Little by little they began to mount; the track wound in and out between great rocks and overhung the streams, becoming here and there so narrow that ten men could stop a thousand; the soldiers marched in Indian file, and wondered why the enemy did not attack in such a favourable place to lay an ambuscade.

But the Tomochitecos, though they knew the Sierra better than any one in Mexico except the Indians, thought it beneath their dignity to leave their town, which they considered sacred, and to defend which all had determined to devote their lives. At one o'clock they halted at La Peña Agujereada,[16] a great rock, and rested till the evening, when once again in the bright moonlight they struggled up the track.

The peaks and needles of the rocks shone in the moonbeams like great organ-pipes. The precipices looked more awful, and the tired men, footsore and carrying their provisions on their backs, stumbled along, oft falling like the Christian on life's track, and oft blaspheming as they fell, as even Christians will when obstacles and pitfalls bar the way. The frightened horses' eyes gleamed bright as phosphorus, as most unwillingly they picked their way, choosing each footstep and snorting wildly now and then as they passed torrents, or the pine boughs waved like phantoms in the night.

They camped at Río Verde, more than half way, with great precautions, fearing a surprise; but nothing happened, and the night passed quietly away.

The next day's journey from Río Verde to Las Juntas only took three hours, and left them but two leagues to march before they reached the town.

Though short, the march was mortal, as it was all uphill and through a country where they could get no water, so that, as usually occurs, they were tired out before the fight began, and lay about the fire wrapped in their blankets sleeping like marmots; but still the enemy did not attack them, so they slept on till nearly daybreak, when the sergeants wakened them silently and prepared them for the fray.

The cold was glacial as the men stood in the ranks waiting until the sun rose, for the guides were not quite certain of the direction of the town. A black descent yawned right in front of them, into which they plunged. Scouts were thrown out, and in the semi-dark they stumbled down the trail, till the stars paled and all the sky grew white. The dawn, scarlet and orange coloured, showed them they had come to a small open space, whence once again the rough track mounted to the clouds. There all the officers dismounted, leaving their horses with the rear-guard, and the men set themselves for the last and steepest climb up the rough road which ran through pine woods which closed black above their heads. The officers, who all had left their kepis with the baggage, had put on grey felt hats with but a strip of bright red ribbon to distinguish them.

Mercado, like the rest, marched silently, feeling the tightening at the stomach which creeps over most men when in peril of their lives, and hoping that the soldiers could not guess his feelings, when suddenly some desultory shots were heard, and the scouts fell back in confusion and the quick-firing gun advanced. Once more the path descended, and they heard but could not see the enemy. Shouts of "Long live the power of God!" "Long live the Blessed Virgin!" and of "Death to Lucifer!" resounded from the recesses of the pine woods and the rocks.

The soldiers, taken at disadvantage, could not see where to direct their fire, and suddenly a man close to Mercado's side opened his arms, let fall his rifle, and with an "Ay, Jesús!" fell dead, remaining open-mouthed with a thin streak of blood staining his dark blue tunic and trickling down into the sand. Then there stepped out from underneath the pine trees a tall figure with a steeple-crowned straw hat, and standing on a rock shouted his war-cry of "Long live the power of God!" and firing rapidly in quick succession, killed three soldiers and struck the bugle from the bugler's mouth. It fell with a dull clang upon the stones, and the heroic fanatic, pierced by a dozen bullets, subsided slowly from his rock, his rifle rolling down the hill close to Mercado's feet.

The column of the troops, attacked on every side by enemies they could not see, slowly retreated with considerable loss, leaving on every side their dead and dying, and at length in great confusion returned to camp, just where they started from some hours ago.

All the time that the fight was taking place, Cruz Chaves, full of religious ardour or fanaticism, for ardour and fanaticism are terms which interchange on victory or defeat, was fortifying to the best of his ability the town which he imagined that he held against the world, for God.

His own house was a veritable fort, entrenched with lines of loopholes pierced for musketry.

In it there lived his brothers José and Manuel with all their families. Built of adobes of the hardest make, a tangle of barbed wire and a strong palisade encircled it. Between it and two other blockhouses, in one of which were kept some fifty prisoners taken in former fights, stood a pedestal of white-washed stone, a cross with linen streamers floating from its arms. The other blockhouse served as a store for arms and cartridges, and close behind it stood a little oratory which also was the study and the bedroom of Cruz Chaves, the self-appointed prophet and the priest of the community.

As he sat by the fire drinking his coffee and meditating on his plans, Bernardo entered, having ridden all the night to bring his news of the advance upon the place. Rising, he said, "It does not matter, for none can strive against the soldiers of the Lord. God will protect us, let us go and pray." Prayer without whisky probably was not much to Bernardo's taste, but silently he followed Cruz down a small winding stair which came out at the church. The porch was full of men, their rifles in their hands, their cartridge-belts all full, all dressed in deerskin or in velveteen. Their hats were felt or straw, high in the crown and heavy, and round them they wore the heavy sausage-shaped silver bands, known as toquillas, which all Mexicans affect.

Those who were seated on the steps arose respectfully as Cruz drew near. Tall and majestic-looking, his wandering eyes and matted hair gave him the look with which convention has endued the prophet, and which is not uncommon in a lunatic asylum.

He walked across the tombstones which formed the flooring of the porch, his deerskin moccasins dulling his footsteps, and giving him an air of mystery as he seemed to glide without a sound.

Entering the aisle, his hat upon his head, he went up to the altar, and turning round towards the body of the church, waited until his followers came in and ranged themselves.

When all had entered, he took up his parable. "Brothers in Jesus Christ and in His Mother, prepare yourselves, confident in the great power of God, to fight the impious sons of Lucifer who are advancing to destroy us and impose their laws. They treat us all as beasts; they take away our saints, our money, and now our Government is sending soldiers here to kill us all. But we fight for God's kingdom, and we cannot die. If we fall wounded and appear as dead, we shall arise again, as did our Lord, on the third day; we shall all conquer by the great power of God."

He paused, and an amen low and intense ran through the church. Outside, the women and the children looked through the porch as horses grazing on the Essex marshes gaze at a hay-barge floating down the tide. Then, taking from the pocket of his blouse some papers, he untied them, and, altering his tone, began to read his disposition for the fight. Then once again resuming a sacerdotal tone, and raising up one hand, he said, "Kneel down," and stood a moment motionless, fixing the people with a glance of steel.

All knelt except Bernardo, till Cruz looked towards him frowning, when he turned pale and fell upon his knees.

Lastly Cruz blessed the company in God's name and that of all the Trinity combined. In silence the fanatics left the church, and Cruz remained to draw up with his officers the plan of the attack which had forced back the troops.

The women had the task assigned of making loopholes, baking tortillas, preparing lint, and making rations of *pinole* and *tasajo* for the men.[17]

At six o'clock all the men capable of bearing arms drew up before his house, where he examined all their rifles, and then their scapularies and the brass medals which they carried round their necks. The women and the girls went to the church to pass the night in prayer, leaving Cruz Chaves and his family alone. He, after having visited the prisoners, sat down before the fire in his own house, his wife and sisters sitting near, but without daring to address him as he sat.

At eight o'clock he rose and said, "Come, let us pray," and the whole family knelt silently before the battered image of a saint, whilst he poured forth a rhapsody of prayer and praise. This finished, he retired to his own room and shut the door, leaving the women silent and miserable, all gazing at the fire.

A silence that seemed preternatural pervaded everything; even the dogs, which in a frontier town in Mexico render the night harmonious, were all silent, and hearing not a sound, forgot to howl. Silent before the fire the women sat, the wife of Cruz, his sisters, Julia, and some girls chewing the cud of bitterness and smothering down their grief.

Suddenly shots echoed through the hills, and a loud knocking nearly broke down the door. They opened it, and a man wrapped in a blanket, carrying his rifle in his hand, came in and asked for Cruz. Cruz came out of his room and took the stranger into the little oratory which served him for his study, and then heard that more troops were coming from Sonora, and bringing with them more than two hundred Indians, Pimas and Opatas, men known throughout Mexico as famous rifle-shots.

Although he must have known his fate was sealed, taken as he was between two forces, each of which was three or four times larger than his own, yet he gave no sign, but, taking down his rifle, threw his blanket round his shoulders and glided silently out into the night. Passing the cemetery, he came to where his brothers José and Manuel with their followers guarded the road by which the troops were forced to march to the attack. He told them to be ready for an assault at break of day, and he himself remained with the reserve. Just as day broke the forces of the Government advanced behind a cloud of skirmishers composed of Pimas and of Opatas. In spite of all their cunning and experience, Cruz and the men whom he had posted in the church tower and on the house-tops shot them like rabbits as they ran from tree to tree. Men dropped like flies, and if a villager fell wounded into the hands of the fierce Indians, his fate was instant death. In one of their attacks they came upon the miserable "Saint" José Carranza, and shot him instantly. At last a body of the troops, led by the Pima Indians, gained a point from whence they could look down upon the town.

Although night fell leaving the town untaken, yet from that moment it was seen that it was but a mere affair of time.

Mercado, in the camp, seated before the fire, had time to meditate upon the glories of the day. The losses on both sides had been severe, one company returning with but seven men, others without an officer, and dozens of men lay groaning on the ground. Throughout the night the wounded crawled into the camp, leaving long trails of blood upon the stones. Others sat pale and hungry round the fires, their heads tied up in blood-stained bandages. But even those were happy in comparison with the poor wretches who had had to be abandoned in the night. Crushed, shivering with cold, and at the same time burned with thirst, they lay like pheasants wounded in a wood, despairing, feverish, and with their nerves strained to the utmost, waiting the advent of the sierra wolves.

Mercado, who had read of glorious war, was horrified. Was this the trade Napoleon plied? Where was the honour and the fame to come in fighting miserable villagers, who had committed nothing worse than folly, and had refused to pay their taxes to the Government, which only knew of them as taxables, having performed no single function of a government except the sending of its tax collectors at due intervals.

But if the troops were in a miserable plight, what was the situation of Tomochic, full with wounded men, without a doctor, provisions scarce, and crowded all together in the three fortified jacals and in the church? At daybreak thirty wounded soldiers and five officers were sent off to Guerrero under an escort, and from the summit of the dominating plateau the quick-firing gun began to play upon the church and batter at the town.

With the first light, the Pimas and Opatas set off into the woods, and soon the rocks rang with their shots and war-whoops, as, under the thick pines, they massacred the wounded and then took their scalps.

All day the civilising Hotchkiss gun played on the church and town, and from behind the rocks the Indian scouts fired upon any one who dared to leave his shelter and to expose himself. About the valley, cows and sheep, frightened at seeing progress for the first time so near, strayed up and down almost too scared to eat. The Indians now and then shot one for food, the troops for sport and for the pleasure of destruction, so dear to men who go to carry Christianity into a heathen land.[18]

All the next day passed pleasantly enough, the troops watching their field-piece play upon the town. The doctor of the brigade, who was an amateur artilleryman himself, directed all the shots, and when they saw a piece of wall fall in a cloud of dust, he and the general opened a brandy bottle and drank the health of Don Porfirio Díaz, the liberator of his country and the presiding genius on her path towards progress, for by this time a train of mules had brought provisions to the camp. Thus did the people of Tomochic at the same time serve not only as an object lesson to the soldiers of what they in their capacity as men might look for from their Government, if they should choose to have ideas of their own, but gave good sport to the officers and to the solitary scientific man, who in the face of all discomfort was by his shooting demonstrating that his election and his calling both were sure.

It soon became apparent that the people of the town were too much decimated to make more attacks, but still they stubbornly clung to the church and houses, firing occasionally, and sallying out at nights to get provisions from their fields. Water they had inside the town in wells, and in the maize-fields near the houses their miserable cattle strayed, and chickens cackled in the yards of the deserted huts. The general gave orders to send out and burn the crops and huts, and soldiers carrying petroleum cans set them on fire, and then returned beneath the burden of the wretched loot afforded by the place. Chickens and pigs and clothes, some old guitars and saddles, pictures of saints, and goat-skins were the treasures that they bore. This military operation took all day, and as the sun set on the mountain tops the splendid amphitheatre was lighted up by the flames issuing from the burning huts, and the blue smoke hung like a dirty rag against the background of the snow. Just before nightfall the besieging force saw a man let himself down from a housetop in the village and run towards the camp. They fired at him, as did the people of the place, but he escaped, and waving a white handkerchief, came safely to the lines. He proved to be one of the prisoners taken a month ago. Cruz Chaves had proposed to him to take up arms against the Government, and he had done so, hoping to escape.

He had brought the news that almost half of the defenders had been killed, that the Medranos who had acted as lieutenants under Cruz were dead, that Manuel Chaves and many more were badly wounded, and were being cared for by the women of the place.

The church was occupied (he said) by twenty men, and there the bulk of the non-combatants had taken refuge, and that some twenty men were still un-wounded in the house of Cruz. Provisions too were short, and water they could only get at night. Cruz Chaves still kept up his spirits and went about encouraging the rest, comforting the women with his prayers and putting heart into the men by his example and contempt of death. The dead had all been buried secretly by night, so that no one should know exactly how many had been killed.

The prisoners spoke of the fanaticism which animated all the men, and said the women seemed dumbfounded, not knowing why or wherefore they were called upon to die.

The news fell on the troops as rain falls on a dried-up field, comforting them for all that they had undergone.

Grouped round their fires, they sat and watched the burning houses pierce a hole into the overwhelming blackness of the night, and no one gave more thought to the poor people of the place than does a huntsman when a hare screams in her agony as she is torn to pieces by the pack.

Once more at daybreak the quick-firing gun took up its civilising toil, but all it did was to drill holes in the adobe, the calibre being far too small to bring the houses down.

Fatigue parties of soldiers were sent down, out of the range of the defenders of the church, to finish up the work of yesterday. Towards mid-day they returned laden with booty and triumphant. Inside the town the miserable people saw their crops destroyed, their houses burned, and all they held most dear destroyed, but made no sign, firing a shot at intervals when any of the spoilers came too near.

The general and the officers were all indignant at their stubbornness. It seemed like insolence, in men without a uniform, without an officer who had gone through a military school, and ignorant of tactics as they were, to keep in check a force three times as numerous as their own, all duly uniformed, and officered by men who had commissions stamped and signed by the chief magistrate of Mexico.

So must have felt our cavalry in the Transvaal when, from behind the rocks, a band of men looking like chimpanzees and dressed in rusty black stepped out and took their arms, bidding them strip, and leaving them only an eyeglass here and there to veil their nakedness.[19]

Shame, patriotism, duty, or what not had spurred the general to declare that the town must be taken by assault. He might as well have waited until thirst and hunger did their work; but, not unnaturally, a soldier thinks his first duty is to fight, and in this case a red flag fluttering at the top of a tall pine stung him to fury, for nothing moves a reasonable man so much as a new flag.

Tamper but with a flag, change blue for green, add or suppress a cap of liberty[20] or star, adjoin a crown or an heraldic monster of some kind, and your most wise sedate philosopher sees red and longs to slay his fellows, so that the majesty of his own bunting may be vindicated.

Certain it was that something had to be undertaken, for there were telegraphs but two days off, and presidents like to have news about their arms when troops are in the field and when the national standard flutters in the breeze.

Besides, it was but reasonable to try and take the rocky plateau on which stood the town, for if once taken, those in the church could not annoy the soldiers with their fire. So on a splended morning in October, bright and clear, the sun upon the mountain tops glistening like crystal and the last smoke ascending from the smouldering houses mingling with the air, the bugle sounded the advance.

Dirty and ragged, shivering with the cold, the soldiers hurried down the hill, then coming to the final climb, rushed forward, receiving as they went a fire which was converged upon them both from the church and from the house where Chaves and his men were still entrenched. As they advanced, a cross-fire took them in the flank, for Chaves had detached a party to fire behind the rocks, having the instinct of a frontier fighter in his blood, which in such situations makes a man who knows the ground worth twenty soldiers whose fighting has been done in colleges and by arithmetic.

Still they pushed upwards, eager to come to closer quarters, and once more the shouts of "Death to Lucifer!" "Long live the Power of God!" rang in their ears. Wild figures rushed from tree to tree, screaming like Indians, as the Tomochitecos sullenly fell back upon their town.

Mercado marched beside his company, a rifle in his hand, which he fired now and then mechanically. His throat was dry, a taste of powder in his mouth, and all his uniform was smeared with blood. How, he could not explain, but still he stumbled upwards, tripping on the stones and sheltering himself behind the trees.

Soon they came on the bodies of the foe, and the fire slackened, but in front a boyish voice cried shrilly, "Long live the Power of God!" and at each cry a man fell dead beside Mercado as he ran. A soldier then cried out, "I see him; fire all at once," and aimed, but as he spoke a bullet pierced his skull and his brains spattered out over Mercado's boots.

Several men fired, but still the voice cried, "Death to the cropped heads!" "Live the Power of God!" It was the last cry that was heard, for as they ran they came upon the body of a boy not more than fourteen years of age, ill fed and ragged, with a bullet through his head, his eyes wide open, and with his rifle clenched between his hands.

His face was livid and his open mouth showed his white teeth, which seemed to smile at death, whilst a red foam oozed slowly from his lips.

The plateau gained, the soldiers threw themselves behind some rocks to rest, whilst some went round and gathered up the arms under a desultory fire from the church tower and from the house of Cruz, the only buildings which had remained with any one alive. But still the obnoxious and unconstitutional red flag waved from the pine tree, and orders came at any risk to tear it down.

A sergeant and some soldiers rushed out, crouching down almost to the ground to gain the tree, when from a hole behind a rock a gun was thrust, and the sergeant, staggering, fell dead without a sound.

The soldiers rushing on, shortening their rifles and firing as they ran, swarmed round the hole like bees. A captain joined them and was crying, "Stop, the man is wounded," when a gigantic head, the long grey hair flecked here and there with blood, appeared above the ground; a rifle followed, and, a shot echoing, the captain fell dead in an instant on the man he wished to save.

Then with a shout the soldiers dashed into the hole, using their bayonets as if they had been spades.

Miguel, who from a little distance off had seen his captain fall, drew near, and looking down into the hole saw that the mass of bloody broken limbs, grey hair, and entrails had been Bernardo, and stood stupefied, thinking that Julia now was free, but that she still was shut up starving in the town.

The soldiers, worn out with fatigue, lay for the most part round a little stream upon their stomachs, lapping the water as it passed, like dogs, and just as greedily. A sergeant counted the rifles, solemnly arranging them in rows, and like a splash of blood was laid upon a rock the torn red flag which had at last been torn down from the pine.

The plateau taken, nothing but death remained for the fanatical inhabitants grouped in the church and in the house of Cruz. But as the greater part of them were women and young children, the state of desperation of the men is easy to imagine; but to describe it only one of themselves could have essayed the task.

The troops advancing burned the other portions of the town, so that at last only the house of Cruz and the church with its tower were standing, and from them at intervals came desultory shots.

The Hotchkiss gun, brought up to but a hundred yards, fired now and then, but did but little damage beyond raising clouds of dust and keeping the inhabitants fast prisoners in the church.

But whilst the villagers endured the pangs of hunger and of thirst, the troops had been refreshed after their efforts in the cause of patriotism by the arrival of a sutler bringing a load of demijohns of the rough spirit called sotol.

Having lost so many men, the general now determined to burn out the people in the church, which, by the fact of his having taken several stone-built houses near it, had become attackable without much risk to life.

His plan was that the soldiers should gather a quantity of faggots and dry-stalks of maize, and under cover of the quick-firing gun rush from the stone-built houses to the church porch, where they would be too near for the men posted in the tower to do much damage to them. As the church had a timber roof, the plan looked good, as if it once took fire the refugees would be obliged either to stay and be smoked out like bees, or trying to escape, be shot to the last man as soon as they came out.

A little river ran between the encampment and the church. This, as the soldiers passed, exposed them for a moment to a direct fire from the church, but having passed it they could shelter behind rocks. Thus making a diversion, their comrades rushing from the houses could set the church on fire. Excited by the spirit they had drunk, the soldiers hurried on across the river, losing four or five men in the few seconds that it took to cross.

Once safe amongst the rocks, they made their way to the deserted houses, and there prepared their wood, petroleum, and faggots, then sallying out piled them in the church porch, the Hotchkiss gun and the picked party of the Pimas and the Opatas fired on and killed all those who dared to show themselves upon the roof or tried to fire from any of the windows of the church.

Soon flames burst from the porch and a dense pall of smoke enveloped everything. But from the roof shouts of "Long live the Power of God!" "Long live the Blessed Virgin!" still were heard, and from the door three or four desperate men, their hair ablaze and firing as they ran, leaped out and burst a path to safety through the soldiers to the fields of maize. More would have followed, but the church door falling from out its hinges interposed a barrier of flame. As the church burned the troops advanced under the cover of the smoke and took position to attack the house in which Cruz Chaves and his men still sullenly held out. All stood and watched the church burn, horrified, knowing that it was full of women and of children who would all perish with the men. So thick became the smoke that nothing could be seen, only long lines of sparks shot out like fireflies in the dark.

Then for a moment came a shift of wind, and from their camp the soldiers saw a woman climb to the topmost of the burning tower and heard her shriek, "Long live the Power of God!" and jump down into the body of the blazing church. Next came a sound as of a powder factory blowing up, as the roof fell and after it the tower.

Then silence, and long columns of thick smoke, jewelled with sparks, shot up into the sky.

Nothing was left of what had been the little mountain town except the house of Cruz with its three tiers of loopholes and its red flag floating defiantly above the roof. Long tongues of fire still shot up from the church, and now and then beams fell with a loud crash which echoed through the valley, and now and then a dropping shot came from the still untaken house where Cruz held out, determined to give up his life and those of all his people to what he thought the greater glory of the Lord. The house was built so solidly that the quick-firing gun had no effect upon it. It was protected from a rush by barricades, and its position was stronger far than had been that of the demolished church, as it commanded all the roads which led to it, standing upon a rocky eminence without a rock or tree for yards on every side.

The general judged that it would cost too dear to take it by assault, and with a soldier's eye he saw that the position had, by its very strength, defects which made its capture but a work of time.

Bare and exposed as the house stood, now that the others had been burned, it was impossible for those inside to get at water but by cover of the night.

So, certain of his prey, the general gave orders to his men to retire out of range, and, having posted sentinels, sat down patiently to wait. But as a measure of precaution, and being probably a man of scientific mind, he had the bodies of the dead defenders of the town dragged, by night, underneath the walls of the beleaguered house, hoping thereby to strike despair and terror or perchance to spread a plague amongst the people all closely packed together and without provisions in the place. Next day one of the prisoners Cruz had taken got away and crawled into the camp, but so reduced by hunger that it was several hours before he could give any information of what was passing in the doomed house upon the rocks. A little later, rising from a bush like an Apache Indian, right in the middle of the space, appeared a woman, who tottered towards the tents. She proved to be of about eighty years of age, bent, grey, and starving, and said that Cruz had let her go, and she had lain all night hidden behind the bush, fearing to get into the line of fire, as bullets passed above her head at intervals.

The general, either from a wish to spare his men or being touched when he thought of the state of things inside the house, where dead and dying, live men and children, all without food or medicine, were huddled close, without a hope but of releasing death, prevailed upon the crone to go back with a message to the chief.

After a thousand vacillations she consented, and hobbled off carrying a letter from the general to Cruz. It called on him for unconditional surrender of the place on pain of being taken by assault and executed with all the male defenders of the town.

The women and children he gave leave to come out to the camp, and promised them a pardon and security. In half an hour the old woman hobbled back, the soldiers crowding to look at her as if she was some strange sort of wild beast. Cruz had refused the terms, and sent to say that he and all the men preferred to die, and that he doubted if the women and children would be safe. Once more the messenger went back to assure him of the general's good faith. Then Cruz decided to let out the women and children, all except his own and several others who had elected to stay and perish with their relations and their friends.

The general was dumbfounded, being really touched or fearing what the newspapers would say. However, nothing remained to him but to go on to the end.

Then from the door of the doomed house issued a train of spectres dressed in rags, their faces livid and their legs so weak that they could scarcely totter through the stones. Torn petticoats and ragged shawls covered their misery; their eyes were downcast, and a low murmuring of sobs and groans came from their thirst-burned mouths.

The soldiers, who had crowded up to gaze, were stupefied: some crossed themselves, and others muttered, turning away to hide their tears. They opened out respectfully and made a way for the appalling troop of famine-stricken wretches silently to pass.

An old bowed, white-haired man came first, leaning upon the shoulder of a girl, thin and discoloured, and with her head bound up in dirty bandages through which appeared a dark and bloody stain. After them came a crone whose face was bloody with an unbandaged wound upon her head. One woman walked erect, carrying a sobbing child, reduced by hunger, but still unsubdued and stoical.

A group of girls whose faces had been handsome before that famine set its mark upon them, wrapped up in gaily coloured tattered shawls and Indian blankets with large black and scarlet checks, staggered along holding each other's hands.

Then came a boy, about six years of age, with the blood dripping from his leg, who limped and sobbed a little as he walked. Next came the mass of misery, a wave of human jetsam which had almost lost humanity. Bent bodies, staring great black eyes, long ragged locks of hair, and dirty flesh showing blue and livid through their rags, they looked like faces in a nightmare; and last of all hobbled the crone who had been ambassadress, babbling and talking to herself, and stopping now and then to stoop and pick a flower or pluck some grass to nibble like a beast.

Miguel Mercado looked intently at the miserable band to see if Julia was amongst them, but, as he could not see her, it apeared that she was one of those who had remained to die with the last faithful few within the town. His task was made the harder as nearly all the women covered up their faces with rags or dirty handkerchiefs, not wishing to be seen in all their misery.[21]

But little now remained to make the triumph of the law complete. From the last house no shots were fired, and not a sign of life apeared but the obnoxious flag still floating in the breeze. The cattle strayed through the deserted maize-fields, the chickens roosted in the trees, and pigs went in and out the houses and devoured the flesh of those who but a day or two ago had been their masters and now lay rotting in the sun. The general saw that the besieged must try to sally out by night to get provisions and draw water from the stream, so, having set his guards round about the watering places and in the fields, he sullenly retired into his tent. The moon rose bright and cold, for at that season of the year and at that altitude the nights were piercing, and the soldiers, wrapped in their greatcoats with blankets over all, were almost freezing at their posts.

All night at intervals the bugles sounded, echoing from post to post, carrying despair into the hearts of the besieged, or perhaps filling them with hope; for those who die for an idea, however foolish, commonly die cheerfully, thus taking their revenge upon the world. At midnight, after the moon had set and a profound and pitchy darkness reigned, the sentinels descried some phantom forms approach the river's edge. They fired at once, and the echoes of the hills indefinitely multiplied the sound, so that it seemed a hidden battle in the obscurity and terror of the night. The Pima Indians stood to arms at once, and gliding through the rocks and shrubs like snakes, found nothing at the river but some jars of water which the heroic martyrs of the "Great Power of God" had filled and hoped to have been able to take back into their fort. Their villainy having been checked, nothing of further note occurred that night, except that the women and the children who had been taken prisoners disturbed the soldiers' rest a little with their untimely lamentations and their coughs. Next day a band of soldiers crawling through the rocks were able to approach the barn where Cruz had all his prisoners, without being seen and fired upon, for the beleaguered Tomochitecos gave no sign of life.

Getting as far as possible beneath the loopholes of the fort, they broke a way into the barn and led the prisoners out and back into the camp. They found that two of them had died of thirst. The rest included a lieutenant and some thirty men, all much reduced by hunger and by cold. During the whole time occupied in getting out the prisoners the fort had never fired a shot. But though they gave no sign of their activity, every one knew that they were ready and determined, and that to rush the place might cost the lives of many soldiers; and besides, a feeling of compassion, mixed with a real admiration of their bravery, had touched the general. All day he walked about before his quarters, not speaking, except now and then to ask the doctor how long he thought the besieged could hold out without water, and then towards evening sent another messenger to Cruz.

Amongst the Pima Indians was an old chief called *Chabolé*. One of the old time Indian hunters, he had traversed all the Sierra Madre of Chihuahua and Sonora more than a hundred times. In better days he had known Chaves well, and had with him taken up mules to sell upon the frontiers of the United States.

Calling him up, the general asked him, "*Chabolé*, would you dare take a message to Cruz Chaves in his house?" "Yes, general," he answered; "God bless me, why not?"

Then taking up a bottle of sotol, he left his rifle leaning against a wall and quietly stepped down into the path towards the stronghold which hitherto had been the road to certain death.

The soldiers watched him near the strong stockade, expecting at each instant to hear a shot and see him fall; but nothing happened, the door was opened, and he quietly disappeared into the house. In twenty minutes he returned unharmed, whistling an habanera softly as he walked. He came up to the general, saluted, and laconically said, "They will hold out till God reclaims their souls."

It seemed that on arriving at the palisade the men inside had shouted, "What is it that you want? Long live the Power of God!" He, without answering them, had called out, "Cruz, Cruz, do you hear? I am come to give you an embrace, a drink, and to ask you to surrender." "Come in," they cried. He went into the gate and found himself in darkness, and heard a voice say, "Shake hands, and let me have the drink." They shook hands in the dark, and Cruz, taking the bottle, drank a little, and then taking his old friend by the shoulders pushed him gently out, saying, "Go and tell them that we do not surrender but to God."

The evening set in with an icy wind, and about sunset one of the rescued prisoners was found to have fired upon the troops when in the power of Cruz. Without delay they took him to a fire and shot him, and his body then was cast into a bonfire which the general had been obliged to light to burn the slain, as the whole camp was rendered pestilential by the stench which was exhaled by the dead rotting bodies torn to pieces by the swine.

Justice thus done and duty vindicated, for it is known that a live traitor smells at least as bad as any traitor dead, the troops disposed themselves to pass the night with the best grace they could, as at the break of the day the general had determined that the place was to be taken by assault. The odour of the burning bodies tainted the air; no sound was heard, but now and then beams of the smouldering church and bits of wall fell suddenly, and a thin penetrating rain wetted the sentinels and made them miserable as they passed slowly to and fro. It seemed as if in the drear sadness of the night that man had challenged his Creator and had wished to show Him that he too could make a hell.

At daybreak all the men assembled round great fires, stamping their feet and drying their wet clothes. At ten o'clock the soldiers, carrying faggots and dry straw, advanced to the attack. Once more the Hotchkiss gun, brought to short range, belched forth its bullets, and with a cheer the soldiers rushed the palisades.

For the last time the cry "Long live the Power of God!" came from the doomed Tomochitecos, and then three soldiers climbing on the roof broke through a hole with bayonets, and as an officer tore down the flag, they flung the lighted faggots and the straw into the body of the house. The men inside fired up the chimney once or twice, and then flames bursting from the windows drove the soldiers to the ground. Their patriotic task was over, the majesty of law avenged, and the triumphant bugle, like the morning cock, crowed cheerfully over the scene of ruin and of death.

An officer on horseback galloped up hastily with orders from the general to save the women and to bring out the suffocating men and shoot them instantly.

Soldiers with litters, which might as well have been called biers, penetrated with difficulty into the horror of the burning house.

They came out carrying bundles of rags and human flesh, some living and some dead, out of what Heriberto Frías calls "that ambient of hell." Most of the living died as soon as they came out and breathed fresh air; others, half-dying, looked at their conquerors with glassy eyes, and some who just could stand menaced the soldiers with their scorched and wounded arms, and mumbled out their war-cry, setting out their faith in the fallacious Power of God, with their lips blistered and blackened by the flames.

All were as thin as skeletons, and on their bones hung bloody, powder-darkened rags.

Not one of them could walk more than a step or two, for, though some few had passed the horrors of the siege without a wound, hunger and thirst had brought them almost to death's door. The bodies which the soldiers brought out of the burning house were thrown at once into a bonfire, which blazed and spluttered and sent out greasy sparks. The seven survivors who were destined to be shot were laid face upwards in a doorway which the fire had spared. Amongst them was a woman, whose blackened and scorched hands still held a rifle bent and twisted with the heat.

Her breast was bare, and over it an empty bandolier was strapped. She was the wife of one of Cruz's brothers, and as they laid her down she murmured, "Long live the Power of God!" and died, her eyes remaining open and her jaw falling almost on her breast.

Beside her was laid Cruz, with an arm bound up in a blue bandage dripping blood, his right leg shattered by a rifle-ball.

Bareheaded as he lay, reduced by want and watching, his masses of black hair and jetty beard, with his pale face and air of resignation, made him a model from which a painter might have taken Christ.

The general, plagued again with goads of conscience or that humanity which often is the soldier's bane, shut himself in his tent and sent the doctor to represent him at the final scene.

When all was ready, the dying men were taken out into an open space.

Cruz asked to be placed next his brother, which was done.

One who could hardly speak begged Cruz to give him a scapulary which he wore about his neck, which all thought had magic powder in it which could restore a man to life. "Give it to him," said Cruz, and the man held it to his lips. Then a young officer with the firing-party drew up his men.

"Kneel," he called out in trembling tones; but none could do so except Cruz.

Advancing till their rifles about touched the dying men, the soldiers fired, and all fell dead but one, Cruz falling like a stone, shot through the heart, his great black eyes remaining open wide and fixed, as if he looked into eternity.

The last man, wounded horribly, was writhing on the ground when he received another bullet, struggled to his knees, and shouted, "Long live the Power of God!" and fell, a bundle of black, blood-stained rags, upon the ground.

Of the one hundred men of Tomochic fit to bear arms none had escaped, and of a thousand soldiers only four hundred now remained.

About a hundred women and some children had been spared, and the great cause of progress and humanity had gained a step. The troops remained a night encamped on what had been the plaza of the town, to rest and celebrate their victory.

Early next morning they set out, and looking back saw nothing standing of the doomed town but a few huts and the still smoking ruins of the church.

The Sierra Madre stood out blue and flecked with snow; the pine woods formed a black and threatening mass; and in the foreground, under a pile of wood, the bodies smouldered, whilst the swine, grunting in the ashes, tore the half-burned flesh of their dead owners, and a thick, nauseating smoke ascended up on high.

NOTES

1. From *Progress* (London: Duckworth, 1905). Not previously published.
2. This was his American journalist friend Frederick R. Guernsey with whom he corresponded regularly between 1901 and 1906. When he first wrote to Graham on 26 October 1901 he already had been in Mexico for sixteen years, presumably with the *Mexican Herald*, as he was in the early 1900s. The title of the book was *Tomochic*, or *Tomóchic*, as Guernsey consistently called it, using the alternative and more old-fashioned spelling. Graham had asked Guernsey to obtain it in late 1902, and was acknowledging receipt of it in 1903, besides suggesting that Guernsey translate it, a proposition that the latter declined, citing laziness as his reason. Graham's version of the novel, as

depicted in "Progress," was praised, but summarily, by Guernsey in
a letter dated 25 July 1905: "You adapted admirably *Tomóchic* which
is strong stuff."

3. Heriberto Frías (1870-1925). Astonishingly, Guernsey, in a letter to
   Graham dated 13 February 1906, states: "Heriberto Frías, author of
   Tomóchic, is dead, pobrecito. A real talent his."

   One of the merits of the novel, which was first published in the
   newspaper *El Demócrata* in 1893, and reprinted in many editions, is
   the accuracy of its observed reality — not surprising since Frías was a
   lieutenant in a batallion that was sent to the village to put down the
   rebellion. He went on to publish other works strongly critical of
   society under corrupt dictatorship, and in this sense prefigures not
   only the uprising itself but the "novel of the Revolution."

4. Olivia's steward in Shakespeare's *Twelfth Night* who, at the instigation of
   the jokers Sir Toby Belch and Sir Andrew Aguecheek, wore a pair of
   curiously cross-gartered yellow stockings to impress and show his
   love for his mistress.

5. Piffaro, or piffero, is a small flute or kind of oboe. The players of this
   instrument are generally called pifferari.

6. *Vie de Jésus* (1863) of Ernest Renan (1823-92), French historian, Hebrew
   scholar and critic, was the first volume of his long-projected work,
   Les Origines du Christianisme (1863).

   Obviously Hugh Conway, pseudonym of the popular British
   novelist John Frederick Fargus (1847-85), author of best-selling
   works like *Called Back* (1883), *A Cardinal Sin* (1883), *Dark Days*
   (1884), and the like. There is no novel or collection of stories called
   My Mother, as this translation is entitled, though one knows that her
   premature death during Fargus's childhood affected him greatly. *Mi
   Madre* may be the changed Spanish title of something like *A Family
   Affair* (1885), for example.

   Mademoiselle Giraud, Ma Femme (1870), the risqué, if not
   pornographic, novel of Adolphe Belot (1829-90), French dramatist
   and novelist.

7. *María* (1867), the Romantic novel *par excellence* of the Colombian Jorge
   Isaacs (1837-95).

8. The old Aztec name for what is now Mexico City.

9. Saint Teresa of Avila (1515-82), the Spanish mystic, whose life was written
   by Gabriela.

10. Athanasius, 4th century A.D., Greek father of the Church and patriarch of
    Alexandria, who held to the doctrine that the Son is of the same
    substance as the Father.

11. Exactly the same message of Antonio Conselheiro, the religious fanatic of
    the aforementioned Graham work, *A Brazilian Mystic* (1920).

12. This is precisely the same description that one finds in the South American
    sketches of the *vizcacha*, the hare-like animal of the pampas of
    Argentina.

13. "This she could do without indiscretion, as she is colonel of artillery in
    Spain" (Graham's footnote).

14. Oman is roughly the coastal region of the eastern part of the Arabic
    peninsula, bounded by the Persian Gulf, the Gulf of Oman and the
    Arabic Sea. El Wahab, or Abd-el-Wahhab (1691-1787), was a
    Muslim reformer whose sect (the Wahabi or Wahabee) flourished in
    central Arabia.

15. "'Salitrose,' which is my adaptation of the Spanish word 'salition' [?]. seems to me a better word than the English 'salitrinous' " (Graham's footnote). "Salition," which means "leaping," might have been transcribed wrongly [salited?], for it makes no sense here. The Spanish word is "salitroso," hence Graham's "salitrose," which in fact was already in use and not coined by Graham.

16. The Perforated Rock.

17. "*Pinole* is a sort of flour made of ground maize, sugar, and cinammon. It is very sustaining, as the writer happens to know" (Graham's footnote).

18. "If I should chance to have readers, they may remember the conduct of the European troops in China three years ago" (Graham's footnote).

19. Graham's reference to the Boer War in South Africa at the turn of the century, an operation which he opposed bitterly as yet another example of unwarranted British imperialist intervention.

20. "Students have often remarked the similarity of the cap of liberty to a nightcap, but have not been able to give any reason for the cause. It may be that the cap of liberty is symbolic of the fact that man is only free in bed" (Graham's footnote).

21. In fact, in his search for Julia amongst the dead and the rubble, Mercado comes across a wounded woman amongst the survivors. Not surprisingly, she turns out to be Julia, who soon dies in the arms of her beloved Miguel.

EDITOR'S PREFACE

"A Hegira" is, in a sense, a companion piece to Gabriela's "The Waggon-Train." He takes over in Mexico City where she leaves off, and describes the Grahams' return trip from Mexico to San Antonio after the cotton-selling fiasco, Robert's fencing stint, and Gabriela's teaching experiences. Graham takes as his focus the six Apaches, whose capture had been indicated by Gabriela, and describes the condition of the Grahams and their companions in contrast with the plight of the fugitive Indians, now escaped from their Mexican prison, and also trying to make their way back home to the Texas border.

I have placed the sketch in this position to give some idea of the hardships which the Grahams had to endure on their return trip to San Antonio. It obviously fits the geographical and chronological pattern that I suggested in the Introduction. Since, in terms of the literary situation, the sketch was written at a slightly earlier period, one can detect a difference in tone. Composed more in the ironic and satiric mood of "Un Pelado," it reflects something of Graham's growing bitterness (cf. the Scottish sketches of the same period). However, one also is aware of the fact that it is a "controlled" bitterness which pervades this sketch in that he is *consciously* writing a literary piece, and not just a letter to the press. His three letters to the *Daily Graphic* of ten years before underline the difference in tone, indicating Graham's awareness of the distinction that an artist has to make in the depiction of such events — another pointer to the growing maturity of Graham as a writer.

A HEGIRA[1]

The giant cypresses, tall even in the time of Montezuma,[2] the castle of
Chapultepec upon its rock (an island in the plain of Mexico), the panorama of
the great city backed by the mountain range; the two volcanoes, the
Popocatepetl and the Ixtaccihuatl, and the lakes; the tigers in their cages, did
not interest me so much as a small courtyard, in which, ironed and guarded, a
band of Indians of the Apache tribe were kept confined. Six warriors, a woman
and a boy, captured close to Chihuahua, and sent to Mexico, the Lord knows
why;[3] for generally an Apache captured was shot at once, following the frontier
rule, which without difference of race was held on both sides of the Río Grande,
that a good Indian must needs be dead.

Silent and stoical the warriors sat, not speaking once in a whole day,
communicating but by signs; naked except the breech-clout; their eyes
apparently opaque, and looking at you without sight, but seeing everything;
and their demeanour less reassuring than that of the tigers in the cage hard by.
All could speak Spanish if they liked, some a word or two of English, but no one
heard them say a word in either tongue. I asked the nearest if he was a
Mescalero, and received the answer: "Mescalero-hay," and for a moment a
gleam shone through their eyes, but vanished instantly, as when the light dies
out of the wire in an electric lamp. The soldier at the gate said they were brutes;
all sons of dogs, infidels, and that for his part he could not see why the *gobierno*
went to the expense of keeping them alive. He thought they had no sense; but in
that showed his own folly, and acted after the manner of the half-educated man
the whole world over, who, knowing he can read and write, thinks that the
savage who cannot do so is but a fool; being unaware that, in the great book
known as the world, the savage often is the better scholar of the two.

But five-and-twenty years ago the Apache nation, split into its chief
divisions of Mescaleros, Jicarillas, Coyoteros, and Lipans, kept a great belt of
territory almost five hundred miles in length, and of about thirty miles in
breadth, extending from the bend of the Río Gila to El Paso, in a perpetual war.
On both sides of the Río Grande no man was safe; farms were deserted, cattle
carried off, villages built by the Spaniards, and with substantial brick-built
churches, mouldered into decay; mines were unworkable, and horses left
untended for a moment were driven off in open day; so bold the thieves, that at
one time they had a settled month for plundering, which they called openly the
Moon of the Mexicans, though they did not on that account suspend their
operations at other seasons of the year. Cochise and Mangas Coloradas, Naked
Horse, Cuchillo Negro, and others of their chiefs,[4] were once far better known

upon the frontiers than the chief senators of the congresses of either of the two republics; and in some instances these chiefs showed an intelligence, knowledge of men and things, which in another sphere would certainly have raised them high in the estimation of mankind.

The Shis-Inday (the people of the woods), their guttural language, with its curious monosyllable "hay" which they tacked on to everything, as "Oro-hay" and "plata-hay"; their strange democracy, each man being chief of himself, and owning no allegiance to any one upon the earth; all now have almost passed away, destroyed and swallowed up by the "Inday pindah lichoyi" (the men of the white eyes), as they used to call the Americans and all those northerners who ventured into their territory to look for "yellow iron." I saw no more of the Apaches, and except once, never again met any one of them; but as I left the place the thought came to my mind, if any of them succeed in getting out, I am certain that the six or seven hundred miles between them and their country will be as nothing to them, and that their journey thither will be marked with blood.

At Huehuetoca I joined the mule-train, doing the twenty miles which in those days was all the extent of railway in the country to the north, and lost my pistol in a crowd just as I stepped into the train, some *lépero* having abstracted it out of my belt when I was occupied in helping five strong men to get my horse into a cattle-truck. From Huehuetoca we marched to Tula, and there camped for the night, sleeping in a mesón built like an Eastern fondak round a court, and with a well for watering the beasts in the centre of the yard. I strolled about the curious town, in times gone by the Aztec capital, looked at the churches, built like fortresses, and coming back to the mesón before I entered the cell-like room without a window, and with a plaster bench on which to spread one's saddle and one's rugs, I stopped to talk with a knot of travellers feeding their animals on barley and chopped straw, grouped round a fire, and the whole scene lit up and rendered Rembrandtesque by the fierce glow of an ocote torch. So talking of the Alps and Apennines, or, more correctly, speaking of the Sierra Madre, and the mysterious region known as the Bolsón de Mapimí, a district in those days as little known as is the Sus to-day, a traveller drew near. Checking his horse close by the fire, and getting off it gingerly, for it was almost wild, holding the hair mecate in his hand, he squatted down, the horse snorting and hanging back, and setting rifle and machete jingling upon the saddle, he began to talk.

"*Ave María purísima*, had we heard the news?" What! a new revolution? Had Lerdo de Tejada reappeared again? or had Cortinas made another raid on Brownsville?[5] the Indios Bravos harried Chihuahua? or had the silver "conduct" coming from the mines been robbed? "Nothing of this, but a voice ran that the Apache infidels confined in the courtyard of the castle of Chapultepec had broken loose. Eight of them, six warriors, a woman and a boy, had slipped their fetters, murdered two of the guard, and were supposed to be somewhere not far from Tula, and, as he thought, making for the Bolsón de

Mapimí, the deserts of the Río Gila, or the recesses of the mountains of the Santa Rosa range."

Needless to say this put all in the mesón almost beside themselves; for the terror that the Indians inspired was at that time so real, that had the eight forlorn and helpless infidels appeared I verily believe they would have killed us all. Not that we were not brave, well armed — in fact, all loaded down with arms, carrying rifles and pistols, swords stuck between our saddle-girths, and generally so fortified as to resemble walking arsenals. But valour is a thing of pure convention, and these men who would have fought like lions against marauders of their own race, scarce slept that night for thinking on the dangers which they ran by the reported presence of those six naked men. The night passed by without alarm, as was to be expected, seeing that the courtyard wall of the mesón was at least ten feet high, and the gate solid ahuehuete clamped with iron, and padlocked like a jail. At the first dawn, or rather at the first false dawn, when the fallacious streaks of pink flash in the sky and fade again to night, all were afoot. Horsemen rode out, sitting erect in their peaked saddles, toes stuck out and thrust into their curiously stamped toe-leathers; their chaparreras giving to their legs a look of being cased in armour, their poblano hats, with bands of silver or of tinsel, balanced like halos on their heads.

Long trains of donkeys, driven by Indians dressed in leather, and bareheaded, after the fashion of their ancestors, crawled through the gate laden with pulque, and now and then a single Indian followed by his wife set off on foot, carrying a crate of earthenware by a broad strap depending from his head. Our caravan, consisting of six two-wheeled mule-carts, drawn by a team of six or sometimes eight gaily-harnessed mules, and covered with a tilt made from the istle, creaked through the gate. The great mesón remained deserted, and by degrees, as a ship leaves the coast, we struck into the wild and stony desert country, which, covered with a whitish dust of alkali, makes Tula an oasis; then the great church sank low, and the tall palm-trees seemed to grow shorter; lastly church, palms and towers, and the green fields planted with aloes, blended together and sank out of sight, a faint white misty spot marking their whereabouts, till at last it too faded and melted into the level plain.

Travellers in a perpetual stream we met journeying to Mexico, and every now and then passed a straw-thatched jacal, where women sat selling atole, that is a kind of stirabout of pine-nut meal and milk, and dishes seasoned hot with red pepper, with tortillas made on the metate of the Aztecs, to serve as bread and spoons. The infidels, it seemed, had got ahead of us, and when we slept had been descried making towards the north; two of them armed with bows which they had roughly made with sticks, the string twisted out of istle, and the rest with clubs, and what astonished me most was that behind them trotted a white dog. Outside San Juan del Río, which we reached upon the second day, it seemed that in the night the homing Mescaleros had stolen a horse, and two of them mounting upon him had ridden off, leaving the rest of the forlorn and miserable band behind. How they had lived so far in the scorched alkali-covered plains, how they managed to conceal themselves by day, or how they steered by night, no one could tell; for the interior Mexican knows nothing of the desert craft, and has no idea that there is always food of some kind for an Apache, either by digging roots, snaring small animals, or at the last resort by catching locusts or any other insect he can find. Nothing so easy as to conceal themselves; for amongst grass eight or nine inches high, they drop, and in an instant, even as you look, are lost to sight, and if hard pressed sometimes escape attention by standing in a cactus grove, and stretching out their arms, look so exactly like the plant that you may pass close to them and be unaware, till their bow twangs, and an obsidian-headed arrow whistles through the air.

Our caravan rested a day outside San Juan del Río to shoe the mules, repair the harness, and for the muleteers to go to mass or visit the poblana girls, who with flowers in their hair leaned out of every balcony of the half-Spanish, half-Oriental-looking town, according to their taste. Not that the halt lost time, for travellers all know that "to hear mass and to give barley to your beasts loses no tittle of the day."

San Juan, the river almost dry, and trickling thirstily under its red stone bridges; the fields of aloes, the poplars, and the stunted palms, its winding street in which the houses, overhanging, almost touch; its population, which seemed to pass their time lounging wrapped in striped blankets up against the walls, was left behind. The pulque-aloes and the sugar-canes grew scarcer, the road more desolate as we emerged into the *tierra fría* of the central plain, and all the time the Sierra Madre, jagged and menacing, towered in the west. In my mind's eye I saw the Mescaleros trotting like wolves all through the night along its base, sleeping by day in holes, killing a sheep or goat when chance occurred, and following one another silent and stoical in their tramp towards the north.

Days followed days as in a ship at sea; the waggons rolling on across the plains; and I jogging upon my horse, half sleeping in the sun, or stretched at night half dozing on a tilt, almost lost count of time. Somewhere between San Juan del Río and San Luis Potosí we learned two of the Indians had been killed, but that the four remaining were still pushing onward, and in a little while we met a body of armed men carrying two ghastly heads tied by their scalp-locks to the saddle-bow. Much did the slayers vaunt their prowess, telling how in a wood at break of day they had fallen in with all the Indians seated round a fire, and that whilst the rest fled, two had sprung on them, as they said, "after the fashion of wild beasts, armed one with a stick, and the other with a stone, and by God's grace," and here the leader crossed himself, "their aim had been successful, and the two sons of dogs had fallen, but most unfortunately the rest during the fight had managed to escape."

San Luis Potosí, the rainless city, once world-renowned for wealth, and even now full of fine buildings, churches and palaces, and with a swarming population of white-clothed Indians squatting to sell their trumpery in the great market-square, loomed up amongst its fringe of gardens, irrigated lands, its groves of pepper-trees, its palms, its wealth of flowering shrubs; its great white domes, giving an air of Baghdad or of Fez, shone in the distance, then grew nearer, and at last swallowed us up, as wearily we passed through the outskirts of the town, and halted underneath the walls.

The city, then an oasis in the vast plateau of Anáhuac (now but a station on a railway-line), a city of enormous distances, of gurgling water led in stucco channels by the side of every street, of long expanses of adobe walls, of immense plazas, of churches and of bells, of countless convents; hedged in by mountains to the west, mouth of the *tierra caliente* to the east, and to the north the stopping-place for the long trains of waggons carrying cotton from the States; wrapped in a mist as of the Middle Ages, lay sleeping in the sun. On every side the plain lapped like an ocean, and the green vegetation round the town stopped so abruptly that you could step almost at once from fertile meadows into a waste of whitish alkali.

Above the town, in a foothill of the Sierra Madre about three leagues away, is situated the "Enchanted City," never yet fouled by the foot of man, but yet existent, and believed in by all those who follow that best part of history, the traditions which have come down to us from the times when men were wise, and when imagination governed judgment, as it should to-day, being the noblest faculty of the human mind. Either want of time, or that belittling education from which few can escape, prevented me from visiting the place. Yet I still think if rightly sought the city will be found, and I feel sure the Mescaleros passed the night not far from it, and perhaps looking down upon San Luis Potosí cursed it, after the fashion that the animals may curse mankind for its injustice to them.

Tired of its squares, its long dark streets, its hum of people, and possessed perhaps with that nostalgia of the desert which comes so soon to all who once have felt its charm when cooped in bricks, we set our faces northward about an hour before the day, passed through the gates and rolled into the plains. The mules well rested shook their bells, the leagues soon dropped behind, the muleteers singing "La Pasadita," or an interminable song about a *gachupín* who loved a nun.[6]

The Mescaleros had escaped our thoughts — that is, the muleteers thought nothing of them; but I followed their every step, saw them crouched round their little fire, roasting the roots of wild mescal; marked them upon the march in a single file, their eyes fixed on the plain, watchful and silent as they were phantoms gliding to the north.

Crossing a sandy tract, the capataz, who had long lived in the Pimería Alta, and amongst the Maricopas on the Gila, drew up his horse and pointing to the ground said, "Viva México! — look at these footmarks in the sand. They are the infidels; see where the men have trod; here is the woman's print and this the boy's. Look how their toes are all turned in, unlike the tracks of Christians. This trail is a day old, and yet how fresh! See where the boy has stumbled — thanks to the Blessed Virgin they must all be tired, and praise to God will die upon the road, either by hunger or some Christian hand." All that he spoke of was no doubt visible to him, but through my want of faith, or perhaps lack of experience, I saw but a faint trace of naked footsteps in the sand. Such as they were, they seemed the shadow of a ghost, unstable and unreal, and struck me after the fashion that it strikes one when a man holds up a cane and tells you gravely, without a glimmering of the strangeness of the fact, that it came from Japan, actually grew there, and had leaves and roots, and was as little thought of as a mere ash-plant growing in a copse.

At an hacienda upon the road, just where the trail leads off upon one hand to Matehuala, and on the other to Río Verde, and the hot countries of the coast, we stopped to pass the hottest hours in sleep. All was excitement; men came in, their horses flecked with foam; others were mounting, and all armed to the teeth, as if the Yankees had crossed the Río Grande, and were marching on the place. "Los indios! Sí, señor," they had been seen, only last night, but such the valour of the people of the place, they had passed on doing no further damage than to kill a lamb. No chance of sleep in such a turmoil of alarm; each man had his own plan, all talked at once, most of them were half drunk, and when our capataz asked dryly if they had thought of following the trail, a silence fell on all. By this time, owing to the horsemen galloping about, the trail was cut on every side, and to have followed it would have tried the skill of an Apache tracker; but just then upon the plain a cloud of dust was seen. Nearer it came, and then out of the midst of it horses appeared, arms flashed, and when nearing the place five or six men galloped up to the walls, and stopped their horses with a jerk. "What news? have you seen anything of the Apaches?" and the chief rider of the gallant band, getting off slowly, and fastening up his horse, said, with an air of dignity, "At the *encrucijada*, four leagues along the road, you will find one of them. We came upon him sitting on a stone, too tired to move, called on him to surrender, but Indians have no sense, so he came at us tired as he was, and we, being valiant, fired, and he fell dead. Then, that the law should be made manifest to all, we hung his body by the feet to a huisache tree." Then compliments broke out and "Vivan los valientes!" "Viva México!" "Mueran los indios salvajes!" and much of the same sort, whilst the five valiant men modestly took a drink, saying but little, for true courage does not show itself in talk.

Leaving the noisy crew drinking confusion to their enemies, we rolled into the plain. Four dusty leagues, and the huisache tree growing by four cross trails came into sight. We neared it, and to a branch, naked except his breech-clout, covered with bullet-wounds, we saw the Indian hang. Half-starved he looked, and so reduced that from the bullet-holes but little blood had run; his feet were bloody, and his face hanging an inch or two above the ground distorted; flies buzzed about him, and in the sky a faint black line on the horizon showed that the vultures had already scented food.

We left the nameless warrior hanging on his tree, and took our way across the plain, well pleased both with the "valour" of his slayers and the position of affairs in general in the world at large. Right up and down the Río Grande on both sides for almost a thousand miles the lonely cross upon some river-side, near to some thicket, or out in the wide plain, most generally is lettered "Killed by the Apaches," and in the game they played so long, and still held trumps in at the time I write of, they, too, paid for all errors, in their play, by death. But still it seemed a pity, savage as they were, that so much cunning, such stoical indifference to both death and life, should always finish as the warrior whom I saw hang by the feet from the huisache, just where the road to Matehuala bifurcates, and the trail breaks off to El Jarral. And so we took our road, passed La Parida, Matehuala, El Catorce, and still the sterile plateau spread out like a vast sea, the sparse and stunted bushes in the constant mirage looming at times like trees, at others seeming just to float above the sand; and as we rolled along, the mules struggling and straining in the whitish dust, we seemed to lose all trace of the Apaches; and at the lone hacienda or rare villages no one had heard of them, and the mysterious hegira of the party, now reduced to three, left no more traces of its passing than water which has closed upon the passage of a fish.

Gómez Farías, Parras, El Llano de la Guerra, we passed alternately, and at length Saltillo came in sight, its towers standing up upon the plain after the fashion of a lighthouse in the sea; the bull-ring built under the viceroys looking like a fort; and then the plateau of Anáhuac finished abruptly, and from the ramparts of the willow-shaded town the great green plains stretched out towards Texas in a vast panorama; whilst upon the west in the dim distance frowned the serrated mountains of Santa Rosa, and further still the impenetrable fastnesses of the Bolsón de Mapimí.

Next day we took the road for Monterrey, descending in a day by the rough path known as *La cuesta de los fierros,*[7] from the cold plateau to a land of palms, of cultivation, orange-groves, of fruit-trees, olive-gardens, a balmy air filled with the noise of running waters; and passing underneath the Cerro de la Silla which dominates the town, slept peacefully far from all thoughts of Indians and of perils of the road, in the great caravansary which at that time was the chief glory of the town of Monterrey. The city with its shady streets, its alameda planted with palm-trees, and its plaza all decorated with stuccoed plaster seats painted pale pink, and upon which during both day and night half of the population seemed to lounge, lay baking in the sun.

Great teams of waggons driven by Texans creaked through the streets, the drivers dressed in a *défroque* of old town clothes, often a worn frock-coat and rusty trousers stuffed into cowboy boots, the whole crowned with an ignominious battered hat, and looking, as the Mexicans observed, like "pantominas, que salen en las fiestas."[8] Mexicans from down the coast, from Tamaulipas, Tuxpan, Vera Cruz and Guatzecoalcos ambled along on horses all ablaze with silver; and to complete the picture, a tribe of Indians, the Kickapoos, who had migrated from the north, and who occasionally rode through the town in single file, their rifles in their hands, and looking at the shops half longingly, half frightened, passed along without a word.[9]

But all the varied peoples, the curious half-wild, half-patriarchal life, the fruits and flowers, the strangeness of the place, could not divert my thoughts from the three lone pathetic figures, followed by their dog, which in my mind's eye I saw making northward, as a wild goose finds its path in spring, leaving no traces of its passage by the way. I wondered what they thought of, how they looked upon the world, if they respected all they saw of civilized communities upon their way, or whether they pursued their journey like a horse let loose returning to his birthplace, anxious alone about arriving at the goal. So Monterrey became a memory; the Cerro de la Silla last vanishing, when full five leagues upon the road. The dusty plains all white with alkali, the grey-green sage-bushes, the salt and crystal-looking rivers, the Indians bending under burdens, and the women sitting at the cross roads selling tortillas — all now had changed. Through oceans of tall grass, by muddy rivers in which alligators basked, by bayous, *resacas*, and by bottoms of alluvial soil, in which grew cotton-woods, black-jack, and post-oak, with gigantic willows; through countless herds of half-wild horses, lighting the landscape with their colours, and through a rolling prairie with vast horizons bounded by faint blue mountain chains, we took our way. Out of the thickets of mesquite wild boars peered upon the path; rattlesnakes sounded their note of warning or lay basking in the sun; at times an antelope bounded across our track, and the rare villages were fortified with high mud walls, had gates, and sometimes draw-bridges, for all the country we were passing through was subject to invasions of *los indios bravos*, and no one rode a mile without the chance of an attack. When travellers met they zigzagged to and fro like battleships in the old days striving to get the "weather gauge," holding their horses tightly by the head, and interchanging salutations fifty yards away, though if they happened to be Texans and Mexicans they only glared, or perhaps yelled an obscenity at one another in their different tongues. Advertisements upon the trees informed the traveller that the place to stop at was the "Old Buffalo Camp" in San Antonio, setting forth its whisky, its perfect safety both for man and beast, and adding curtly it was only a short four hundred miles away. Here for the first time in our journey we sent out a rider about half-a-mile ahead to scan the route, ascend the little hills, keep a sharp eye on "Indian sign," and give us warning by a timely shot, all to dismount, corral the waggons, and be prepared for an attack of Indians, or of the roaming bands of rascals who like pirates wandered on the plains. Dust made us anxious, and smoke ascending in the distance set us all wondering if it was Indians, or a shepherd's fire; at halting time no one strayed far from camp, and we sat eating with our rifles by our sides, whilst men on horseback rode round the mules, keeping them well in sight, as shepherds watch their sheep. About two leagues from Juárez a traveller bloody with spurring passed us carrying something in his hand; he stopped and held out a long arrow with an obsidian head, painted in various colours, and feathered in a peculiar way. A consultation found it to be

Apache, and the man galloped on to take it to the governor of the place to tell him Indians were about, or, as he shouted (following the old Spanish catchword), "there were Moors upon the coast."[10]

Juárez we slept at, quite secure within the walls; started at daybreak, crossing the swiftly-running river just outside the town, at the first streak of light; journeyed all day, still hearing nothing of the retreating Mescaleros, and before evening reached Las Navas, which we found astir, all lighted up, and knots of people talking excitedly, whilst in the plaza the whole population seemed to be afoot. At the long wooden tables set about with lights, where in a Mexican town at sundown an al fresco meal of kid stewed in red pepper, tamales and tortillas, is always laid, the talk was furious, and each man gave his opinion at the same time, after the fashion of the Russian mir, or as it may be that we shall yet see done during debates in Parliament, so that all men may have a chance to speak, and yet escape the ignominy of their words being caught, set down, and used against them, after the present plan. The Mescaleros had been seen passing about a league outside the town. A shepherd lying hidden, watching his sheep, armed with a rifle, had spied them, and reported that they had passed close to him; the woman coming last and carrying in her arms a little dog; and he "thanked God and all His holy saints who had miraculously preserved his life." After the shepherd's story, in the afternoon firing had been distinctly heard towards the small rancho of Las Crucecitas, which lay about three leagues further on upon the road. All night the din of talk went on, and in the morning when we started on our way, full half the population went with us to the gate, all giving good advice; to keep a good look-out, if we saw dust to be certain it was Indians driving the horses stolen from Las Crucecitas, then to get off at once, corral the waggons, and above all to put our trust in God. This we agreed to do, but wondered why out of so many valiant men not one of them proffered assistance, or volunteered to mount his horse and ride with us along the dangerous way.

The road led upwards towards some foothills, set about with scrubby palms; not fifteen miles away rose the dark mountains of the Santa Rosa chain, and on a little hill the rancho stood, flat-roofed and white, and seemingly not more than a short league away, so clear the light, and so immense the scale of everything upon the rolling plain. I knew that in the mountains the three Indians were safe, as the whole range was Indian territory; and as I saw them struggling up the slopes, the little dog following them footsore, hanging down its head, or carried as the shepherd said in the "she-devil's" arms, I wished them luck after their hegira, planned with such courage, carried out so well, had ended, and they were back again amongst the tribe.

Just outside Crucecitas we met a Texan who, as he told us, owned the place, and lived in "kornkewbinage with a native gal," called, as he said, "Pastory," who it appeared of all the females he had ever met was the best hand to bake "tortillers," and whom, had she not been a Catholic, he would have made his wife. All this without a question on our part, and sitting sideways on his horse, scanning the country from the corner of his eye. He told us that he had "had right smart of an Indian trouble here yesterday just about afternoon. Me and my 'vaquerys' were around looking for an estray horse, just six of us, when close to the ranch we popped kermash right upon three red devils, and opened fire at once. I hed a Winchester, and at the first fire tumbled the buck; he fell right in his tracks, and jest as I was taking off his scalp, I'm doggoned if the squaw and the young devil didn't come at us jest like grizzly bars. Wal, yes, killed 'em, o' course, and anyhow the young 'un would have growed up; but the squaw I'me sort of sorry about. I never could bear to kill a squaw, though I've often seen it done. Naow here's the all-firedest thing yer ever heard; jes' as I was turning the bodies over with my foot a little Indian dog flies at us like a 'painter,' the varmint, the condemndest little buffler I ever struck. I was for shootin' him, but 'Pastory' — that's my 'kornkewbyne' — she up and says it was a shame. Wal, we had to bury them, for dead Injun stinks worse than turkey-buzzard, and the dodgasted little dog is sitting on the grave, 'pears like he's froze, leastwise he hasn't moved since sun-up, when we planted the whole crew."

Under a palm-tree not far from the house the Indians' grave was dug, upon it, wretched and draggled, sat the little dog. "Pastory" tried to catch it all day long, being kind-hearted though a "kornkewbyne"; but, failing, said "God was not willing," and retired into the house. The hours seemed days in the accursed place till the sun rose, gilding the unreached Santa Rosa mountains, and bringing joy into the world. We harnessed up the mules, and started silently out on the lonely road; turning, I checked my horse, and began moralizing on all kinds of things; upon tenacity of purpose, the futility of life, and the inexorable fate which mocks mankind, making all effort useless, whilst still urging us to strive. Then the grass rustled, and across an open space a small white object trotted looking furtively around, threw up its head and howled, ran to and fro as if it sought for something, howled dismally again, and after scratching in the ground, squatted dejectedly on the fresh-turned-up earth which marked the Indians' grave.

NOTES

1. From *Thirteen Stories* (London: Heinemann, 1900). First published in *Saturday Review*, 88 (5 August 1899), 160-64.
2. Moctezuma, the Aztec war chief and emperor at the time of Cortés's subjugation of Mexico, died in 1520.
3. Robert takes up the theme of the Apache prisoners mentioned by Gabriela in "The Waggon Train."
4. May be translated as Red Sleeves and Black Knife.
5. Miguel Lerdo de Tejada (1812-61) was one of the anti-clerical Liberal leaders in Mexico at the time of Benito Juárez's Reform movement in the 1850s and 1860s. Lerdo is best known for his anti-church *Ley Lerdo*, a law which broke up ecclesiastical lands and offered them for sale. Cortinas was one of the last of the Indian marauding chiefs.

6. Graham's footnote on the love of the Spaniard for the nun reads thus: "It had a chorus reflecting upon convent discipline:

> For though the convent rule was strict and tight,
> She had her exits and her entrances by night."

7. Literally "The Hill or the Slope of the Irons." "Fierros" is probably a wrong transcription of "fieros," meaning the wild ones i.e. the Indians. This seems to make more sense to me.

8. "Mimers going out to a fiesta."

9. Graham was fascinated by the Kickapoos, an Indian people originally from Wisconsin, who had now moved down to Oklahoma and Chihuahua. He refers to them in detail on several occasions in his letters to his mother. See my Introduction, p. 13.

10. Given the conquest and occupation of Spain by the Moors from 711 till 1492, when the last of the "infidels" were expelled with the end of the Reconquest, it is not surprising that in early Spanish religious drama in the New World, the Moor was always portrayed as the villain (cf. the stereotyped roles of cowboys and Indians in the traditional Hollywood Western film). When the Spanish priests presented these plays to their Indian charges, the Indian tended to sympathise more with the plight of the "villain," given the white man's treatment of the native people.

EDITOR'S PREFACE

Back in Texas after the commercial loss of the Mexican trip, Graham tried to settle down to several ranching enterprises which all terminated in failure, at least in monetary terms, although they provided him with experience and material that were to be the stuff of his future writings. The main ranching venture failed due to a raid by Indians who destroyed his property, and captured or released his horses and cattle. This seems greatly ironic to us, since Graham, more than most of his contemporaries, sympathised with the plight of the beleaguered North American Indians, and raised both his pen and his voice in their defence — even, it should be added, when he himself was a victim of their barbarous plundering, as in this case.

After the ranching fracas, he took himself off to various parts of Texas and the South West, participating in all kinds of activities related to horses and cattle. Probably at this time he met people like the old German couple of this story who, like many others, including the Grahams, came to the New World, and Texas in particular, full of hope and optimism, desirous of making their fortune and a new life in this "land of oportunity," as the advertising brochures in Europe described it. If, as I suggested earlier, it was the human element that attracted Graham, nowhere is it more obvious than in this sad, poignant tale about loneliness and isolation, dreams and illusions, and memories of what Graham's old friend Hudson called "far away and long ago."

HOPE[1]

Snow had fallen ceaselessly for hours, blotting out all the features of the landscape, but leaving here and there the red earth, bare, upon the trail that led from San Antonio to La Bandera as it wound about between the scrub of huisache and mesquite. It lay congealed upon the half-transparent twigs of the pinched redbuds that looked as miserable as does a ruffled parrot in a cage on a cold winter's day. In the deep hollows horses thrust their muzzles into the powdery snow, and now and then beat at it with their feet impatiently, as if they thought that Nature had played some joke upon them that they found out of place. The Helotes Creek, half frozen, formed the boundary between the post-oak country that stretched out like a natural park and the low plains thick with a scrub of thorny bush. Upon the mound, shaded by a thick grove of dark pecans, a low-eaved house surrounded by a low snake-fence looked down upon the creek.

The unfamiliar snow piled on the roof gave a false air of Northern Europe, which the wild howling of the prairie wolves intensified. Inside and blinking at the fire sat the old Swabian peasants,[2] who had emigrated years ago, and now in their old age had become rich and owned the ranch and the wide range for cattle that ran from the Helotes, to the north fork of the Pipe Creek. Their children, born Americans, had left them when they grew up, and lived, some on the Río Grande, others in Arizona, but all of them thousands of miles away in tastes, in sentiment, and in their view of life. Hard and unsentimental, they had all received that education which their parents lacked, but the old people had preserved their pristine ignorance of modern life and wonder at the world. Gretchen and Hans they had remained to everybody, and spoke a mixture of bad English and their native tongue. They sat and gazed into the fire, and the wreathed snow perhaps had set them thinking on their old home and life, for it was Christmas Eve, and memory stirred in their hearts.

After a silence the old man turned to his wife and said, "Gretchen, to-morrow will be Christmas Day. That Mexican who herd the sheep say it is Noche Puena,[3] just as he saddled up his horse to go to town. It is the night of nights . . . dat night the Kings all come to Bethlehem . . . it set one thinking, eh?"

Gretchen, after a long look in the fire, rejoined, "Yes, lieber Hans, I think of many things — of the old country, of you when you was young . . . myself too, mit my yellow hair, you say was like de gold, and of our life . . . where has it gone to, so long and yet so quick, it seems as yesterday?"

Hans drew his chair across the hearth, and, taking up her hand, patted it tremulously and said, "Ach, I think too of many things; but your hair,

Gretchen, still is golden, for old Hans ... What a night, eh? How de coyotes howl, just like the wolves in Swabia in that long time ago you speak of."

They sat holding each other's hands, till Gretchen said, "To-night the children all put out their shoes for Santa Claus ... you will laugh, but — no, I hardly like to say it — I still have one of the wooden shoes that little Gretchen mit de golden hair was wearing long ago in the old country. . . . What if we put him out?"

The old man ran his hand affectionately over his wife's grey, wiry hair, and pinched her withered, but still rosy cheek, just as he might have done in the far-off time towards which their thoughts were straying on that night.

Rising, he walked across the room and, throwing back the shutter, looked out into the dark. The clump of tall pecans formed a vast snowy dome; in the corral the horses huddled close together with their tails to the blast, owls hooted, and the wind roared amongst the trees. "It is still snowing, and the creek is rising; dat Mexican did well to start for town: in an hour more no one could cross," he said. "If the black schelm was a white man he'd lose the trail to San Antonio and die in the drifts; but, never fear, the devil knows his own. . . . Ah, yes, the shoe, you say — put him out then, little old fool; all we can hope for now is that Santa Claus take us for children and send us something; for what shall we hope for now, eh, little old fool? . . . Well, put him out."

All the time that he had been speaking, his wife had had her head bent over a great box, and now drew out, wrapped in a piece of flannel, an old wooden shoe. She held it tenderly, but half ashamed, just as a savage might have held some fetich in his hands, after conversion to the true faith, before a missionary. Clumsily, but artistically made, somehow, out there on the Helotes Creek, removed from all tradition, and face to face with Nature, it spoke of Europe and of an older world. The pebbles of the village street had dinted it and left impressions of themselves upon the sole, just as life leaves its wrinkles on the face. As the old couple looked at it, unbidden tears rose to their eyes, and Hans stretched out a bony finger and touched it timidly, just as a man touches the face of his first child, half proudly, half in alarm at the new fetter he has forged upon his life. He said, "Ach, Gretchen, your foot was not so big then, back in those days. I tink I hear you now run like a little pony on the street." Taking the shoe, he crossed the room and, opening the door, let in the driving snow with a cold blast that made the cheap petroleum lamp flicker and jump, and set it down outside.

Gretchen had thrown new logs upon the hearth, and, drawing up her chair, said to her husband, "Come and sit down, and let us drink glass beer. I always hope for something, something that come into our life even now and make us happy ... not that we are not happy ... but something wonderful."

Her husband, either impressed by her simplicity — the one thing in the world impressive — or to humour her, answered with a smile, "Ja ... yes, and Santa Claus, he send us something, maybe ... at any rate, to-morrow, if the trails are passable, some of the children will be here." The glare of the great logs,

of hard mesquite, fell on their wrinkled faces as they sat, married by Time,
before the fire. Hans, in a suit of homespun clothes, his trousers tucked into his
boots, with his bald head as shiny as a billiard ball, his grey and tangled beard,
red cheeks, and hands like roots of trees, looked hale and prosperous. His wife, in
her bed-ticking gown confined about the waist with a broad string of tape, her
feet encased in slippers down at heel, and a white cap upon her head, was thin
and angular; and as she sat holding her husband's rugged hand in hers, looked
like a wooden toy, made in Thuringia,[4] in an old-time Noah's ark.

Still there was something spiritual in her face, as if the world and all its
trials, toil, disappointments, and the cares of a large family had left no mark
upon her soul, and as if the wrinkles on her brow were but the work of Time and
went no deeper than the skin.

A German clock, brought from their home across the sea, ticked on the
wall, measuring out time, as it were, in an old-fashioned Swabian way, pausing
a little every now and then and whirring wheezily before it struck the hour. An
air of cleanliness almost unnatural was over everything. The plates and dishes
shone, as if they had been varnished, in the rough wooden rack above the
dresser, and chairs and tables had been beeswaxed over till they appeared to
glow. The air of comfort and of home contrasted strangely with the wild night
and the position of the ranch on the north fork of the Helotes Creek out on the
Texan plains.

Sleep fell upon the couple sitting by the fire, and as they slept the fire
burned low upon the hearth. Outside nothing was heard but the wild seething
of the wind, and now and then a rush as of an avalanche in miniature, as the
snow slid down from the steep roof. An hour or two slipped past, and the storm
moderated. The moon shone brightly, and in the snow the tracks of animals
were seen — the small, round holes that the deer's feet had made, the footsteps
of the wolves like those of a large dog, the bear's flat trail, as if a man had passed
on snowshoes, revealed as on a chart their passage through the storm. The
sleepers stirred uneasily, and then, awakened by the cold, sat up and looked at
one another.

Hans piled fresh logs upon the fire, stamping them in position with his foot,
and then, when they had warmed themselves at the red blaze, said "Did you
dream, Gretchen?" "Yes, Hans," she answered. "I dreamed a lovely dream.
We were both young again and walking in a wood. You take my hand and say,
'Gretchen, I lofe you ... your hair is golden, your lips so red, I want to kiss
them.' ... Oh, it was lovely.... Did you dream, Hans?"

A shadow ran across his face as he replied, "Yes, I dream too. I dream of all
our struggles — how we came to America without a heller, and how we starved
and fought ... of how we slaved, and then of how we build this house. Of our
first son — the one the Indians killed ... of all the rest; and then it seemed I saw
us both sit sleeping here before the fire."

"Oh, Hans!" his wife rejoined, "what for a dream was that? You have not
been asleep." She paused and saw her husband really had dreamed, and then,

smiling a weary smile, said, "Go, *liebling schatz*[5] — this is the way I used to speak to you in the old days — and bring the shoe you put outside the door. I hope that Santa Claus may have put something in it, something wonderful."

Her husband kissed her cheek, and, gained a little by her faith, opened the door and carried in the shoe. Something was in it of a truth, for Santa Claus, who never disappoints people who trust in him, had filled it up with snow. As they stood looking at it ruefully, the long-drawn howl of a coyote sounded far out upon the plain.

NOTES

1. From *Hope* (London: Duckworth, 1910). First published in *Saturday Review*, 109 (5 May 1910), 170-71.
2. Natives of Swabia, a duchy in medieval Germany.
3. i.e. Nochebuena, or Christmas Eve.
4. A region of Central Germany.
5. An old-fashioned term of endearment, translated literally as "darling treasure."

EDITOR'S PREFACE

During his second stay in San Antonio, after the Mexican interlude, Graham, we know, although the letters home tell us remarkably little, was involved in various activities connected with riding and horses. He is supposed to have schooled horses for the rich, if we can believe Tschiffely, and also broken in mustangs. It is claimed that he went on a buffalo-hunting expedition on the Texas plains and he certainly worked with a group driving cattle to and from Mexico and Texas, as this little story illustrates.

This sketch is a good example of his sharp eye and keen ear, which helps to support his reputation as a painter of regional customs. When one remembers that this piece was written almost forty years after the event, one has a greater admiration for Graham's capacity not only to recall but also to immortalise the moments that capture the essence of a way of life or a culture.

It is rather interesting that Graham, then (1916) involved in obtaining horses for the war front on behalf of the British government, should have considered this collection, *Brought Forward*, as his swan song. This apparent retirement from writing prompts the reviewer in the *Nation* (London), XX (21 October 1916), 107-09, to lament that if this is indeed Graham's farewell to literature, it will be a sad loss. Partially true to his word, Graham did not produce anything during the rest of the war, occupied as he was with patriotic work. Fortunately, it was a temporary withdrawal, and by 1920 his books started to re-appear at the rate of almost one a year over the next decade and until his death in 1936.

PREFACE TO
BROUGHT FORWARD[1]

Luckily the war has made eggs too expensive for me to fear the public will pelt me off the stage with them.

Still, after years of writing, one naturally dreads the cold potato and the orange-peel.

I once in talking said to a celebrated dancer who was about to bid farewell to her admirers and retire to private life, "Perhaps you will take a benefit when you come back from finishing your last tour." She answered, "Yes . . ."; and then added, "or perhaps two."

That is not my way, for all my life I have loved bread, bread, and wine, wine, not caring for half-measures, like your true Scot, of whom it has been said, "If he believes in Christianity he has no doubts, and if he is a disbeliever he has none either."

Once in the Sierra Madre, either near the Santa Rosa Mountains or in the Bolsón de Mapimí, I disremember which, out after horses that had strayed, we came upon a little shelter made of withies, and covered with one of those striped blankets woven by the Navajos.

A Texan who was with the party pointed to it, and said, "That is a wickey-up, I guess."

The little wigwam, shaped like a gipsy tent, stood close to a thicket of huisache trees in flower. Their round and ball-like blossoms filled the air with a sweet scent. A stream ran gently tinkling over its pebbly bed, and the tall prairie grasses flowed up to the lost little hut as if they would engulf it like a sea.

On every side of the deep valley — for I forgot to say the hut stood in a valley — towered hills with great, flat, rocky sides. On some of them the Indian tribes had scratched rude pictures, records of their race.

In one of them — I remember it just as if now it was before my eyes — an Indian chief, surrounded by his friends, was setting free his favourite horse upon the prairies, either before his death or in reward of faithful services. The little group of men cut in the stone, most probably with an obsidian arrow-head, was life-like, though drawn without perspective, which gave those figures of a vanished race an air of standing in the clouds.

The chief stood with his bridle in his hand, his feather war-bonnet upon his head, naked except the breech-clout. His bow was slung across his shoulders and his quiver hung below his arm, and with the other hand he kept the sun off from his face as he gazed upon his horse. All kinds of hunting scenes were there displayed, and others, such as the burial of a chief, a dance, and other ceremonials, no doubt as dear to those who drew them as are the rites in a cathedral to other faithful. The flat rock bore one more inscription, stating that Eusebio Leal passed by bearing despatches, and the date, June the fifteenth, of the year 1687. But to return again to the lone wickey-up.

We all sat looking at it: Eustaquio Gómez, Polibio Medina, Exaltación García, the Texan, two Pueblo Indians, and I who write these lines.

Somehow it had an eerie look about it, standing so desolate, out in those flowery wilds.

Inside it lay the body of a man, with the skin dry as parchment, and his arms beside him, a Winchester, a bow and arrows, and a lance. Eustaquio, taking up an arrow, after looking at it, said that the dead man was an Apache of the Mescalero band, and then, looking upon the ground and pointing out some marks, said, "He had let loose his horse before he died, just as the chief did in the picture-writing."

That was his epitaph, for how death overtook him none of us could conjecture; but I liked the manner of his going off the stage.

'Tis meet and fitting to set free the horse or pen before death overtakes you, or before the gentle public turns its thumbs down and yells, "Away with him."

Charles Lamb, when some one asked him something of his works, answered that they were to be found in the South Sea House, and that they numbered forty volumes, for he had laboured many years there, making his bricks with the least possible modicum of straw, just like the rest of us.[2]

Mine, if you ask me, are to be found but in the trails I left in all the years I galloped both on the prairies and the pampas of America.

Hold it not up to me for egotism, O gentle reader, for I would have you know that hardly any of the horses that I rode had shoes on them, and thus the tracks are faint.

NOTES

1. From *Brought Forward* (London: Duckworth, 1916).
2. Charles Lamb (1775-1834), best known for his essays, collected in the celebrated series *Essays of Elia* (1823) and the *Last Essays of Elia* (1833). As a young man he worked as a clerk for both the South Sea Company (1791) and the East India Company (1792).

EDITOR'S PREFACE

Graham, of course, knew well the South Western part of the United States which he has immortalised in his sketches. Not having travelled in the cold regions of the North West, he did not feel competent to write of this area, certainly not in geographical or literary terms. However, he was not averse to taking up cudgels, for political, social or humanitarian reasons, on behalf of the oppressed Indians of the Dakotas, as witnessed by his spirited attack in the three letters to the *Daily Graphic* in the 1890 period.

Although he had met and admired Buffalo Bill (but in the South West) before and after the formation of the latter's horse show, Graham did not consider himself the appropriate writer to capture the life of a man associated with the North West. Don Roberto, however, never forgot Cody, nor Teddy Roosevelt's flattering invitation to keep the colonel's name alive in print. Ten years after Buffalo Bill's death and Graham's regretful decision not to write Cody's biography, this sketch, "Long Wolf," motivated by the discovery of an abandoned grave in London, serves in fact to keep alive the name not only of Cody but of a Sioux Indian chief who was part of Buffalo Bill's show. The circle is complete. Cody is restored to prominence, and the Dakota Indian whom Graham felt unqualified to eulogise, but unafraid to defend, is doubly remembered — by his London tomb and by Graham's sketch. The debt to the North West is finally and irrevocably paid. Read in conjunction with the opening piece, "Three Letters on the Indian Question," this elegiac sketch closes the cycle by making the same point, if less stridently.

One notes the same ambivalence with regard to Western pioneers and the Indians, as one finds in his South American sketches, with respect to the Spanish conquistadores and the indigenous population of the southern continent. Graham admires the human and heroic qualities on both sides, for, after all, he claims, they were both American.

LONG WOLF[1]

Introductory Note By Kermit Roosevelt

My interest in Mr. Cunninghame Graham's writings was first aroused through reading the dedication in Mr. W. H. Hudson's delightful collection of short stories, gathered under the title *El Ombú*.[2] It runs as follows:

TO MY FRIEND

R. B. CUNNINGHAME GRAHAM

("Singularísimo Escritor Inglés")

Who has lived with and knows (even to the marrow as they would themselves say) the horsemen of the Pampas, and who alone of European writers has rendered something of the vanishing colour of that remote life.

My father had been for many years an eager reader of all that Mr. Cunninghame Graham wrote, and I well remember his appreciation of the following letter which he received from him shortly after Buffalo Bill's death:

March 27th, 1917.

Cartagena de Indias,
Colombia.
The Honourable,
Colonel Theodore Roosevelt,

DEAR COLONEL ROOSEVELT:

I saw by chance to-day in *Harper's Magazine* that a national monument is to be raised to my old friend Colonel Cody; that it is to take the form of a statue of himself on horseback (I hope the horse will be old Buckskin Joe), that he is to be looking out over the North Platte, and that you have kindly consented to receive subscriptions for it.

When Cody and I were both young I remember him at the Horsehead Crossing, in or about the year 1880 I think, and subsequently saw him next year with the first germs of his great show in San Antonio de Bexar, Texas. (God bless Western Texas, as we used to say in those days — it is a thirsty land.)

Cody was a picturesque character, a good fellow (I hope the story of his game of poker on his death-bed is not apocryphal), and a delightful figure on horseback. How well I can see him on his beautiful grey horse in the show!

Every American child should learn at school the history of the conquest of the West.

The names of Kit Carson, of General Custer and of Colonel Cody should be as household words to them. These men as truly helped to form an empire as did the Spanish conquistadores.

Nor should Sitting Bull, the Short Wolf, Crazy Horses and Rain-in-the-Face be forgotten.

They too were Americans, and showed the same heroic qualities as did their conquerors.

I would not have Captain Jim of the Modocs fall into oblivion either.[3]

All of these men, and they were men of the clearest grit, as no one knows better than yourself, were actors in a tremendous drama, set in such surroundings as the world never saw before, or will see again.

Anch' io son pittore,[4] that is to say, I too knew the buffalo, the Apaches, and the other tribes of the Río Grande.

May I then trouble you with my obolus, a cheque for £20 towards the national monument to Buffalo Bill?

I envy him his burial-place.

May the statue long stand looking out over the North Platte.

If in another world there is any riding — and God forbid that I should go to any heaven in which there are no horses — I cannot but think that there will be a soft swishing as of the footsteps of some invisible horse heard occasionally on the familiar trails over which the equestrian statue is to look.

Believe me, dear Colonel Roosevelt,

> Yours most sincerely,
> ## R. B. CUNNINGHAME GRAHAM.

P.S. — I congratulate you most heartily on the force which you are raising. It is like you, and if I had been blindfolded and asked who was raising such a force, I should have answered unanimously Teddy Roosevelt.

After eleven months in the Argentine, buying horses for the British Government, I am at present in Colombia on a mission connected with cattle, on the same account.[5]

> R. B. C. G.

I thought at the time that here was the writer that could make Buffalo Bill and his era live and speak and act for our children and our children's children. After the Armistice I made the suggestion, and it was at first favourably received, but upon thinking it over Mr. Cunninghame Graham decided that, since his roaming in North America and participation in our frontier life had been largely confined to our South-West and to Mexico, he did not feel inclined to take up a work which would necessarily deal largely with the bleak frozen winters of the North-West, to which he was a stranger.

Accompanying his final decision, as a grateful earnest of his interest, and appreciation of the West, he sent the following sketch, which, instead of reconciling us to the decision, can only serve to make us regret it the more.

KERMIT ROOSEVELT.

LONG WOLF

In a lone corner of a crowded London cemetery, just at the end of a smoke-stained, Greco-Roman colonnade, under a poplar tree, nestles a neglected grave.

The English climate has done its worst upon it. Smoke, rain, and then more smoke, and still more rain, the fetid breath of millions, the fumes of factories, the reek of petrol rising from little Stygian pools on the wood pavements, the frost, the sun, the decimating winds of spring, have honeycombed the headstone, leaving it pitted as if with small-pox, or an old piece of parchment that has long moulded in a chest.

Upon the stone is cut the name of Long Wolf and an inscription setting forth he died in 1892 in Colonel Cody's Show. Years he had numbered fifty-nine. The legend says he was chief — I think a chief of the Oglala Sioux, if memory does not play me false.

In high relief upon the cross, our emblem of salvation, a wolf is sculptured, the emblem of the tutelary beast he probably chose for himself in youth, during his medicine fast. It may have been that the name grew from some exploit or some incident in early life. Most probably the long wolf meant more to him than did the cross that Colonel Cody has erected over his dead friend and comrade in the wild life they understood so well. If the Long Wolf resents it, they can discuss the matter where they now ride — for that they ride, perhaps some bronco Pegasus, I feel certain, as heaven would be no heaven to them if they were doomed to walk.

From whence the Long Wolf came so far, to lay his bones in the quiet corner of the Brompton Cemetery where now he sleeps, that is to me unknown, as absolutely as the fair field where the fledged bird had flown was to the poet. All that I know is that the bird was fledged, flew for some nine-and-fifty years, and now rests quietly in his forgotten grave.

The tombstones stand up, white in marble, grey in granite, and smoke-defiled when cut in common stone. They stand like soldiers, all in serried rows. The occupiers of the graves beneath them sleep on undisturbed by railway whistle or motor-horn, by blasts of steam, by factory sirens, or the continuous rumble of our Babylon. These were familiar sounds to them in life. If they could wake and should not hear them, their ears would pine for what had filled them all their lives. Upon each stone is set the name and age and virtues of its occupant. A pious text informs the world that a devoted wife and mother died in the sure and certain hope of a glorious resurrection. All charitable folk will hope her faith has been rewarded in the empyrean that she now inhabits, just as her virtue was rewarded here on earth, for to be forty years a devoted wife and mother is its own reward.

A little farther off, a general, his battles over, reposes in his warrior's cloak. He needs it, for the white marble makes a chilly couch in our high latitude. A champion sculler, with his marble boat and broken sculls, has gained his prize. A pugilist is cut in stone in fighting attitude, and farther off there sleeps a publican.

Men, women, children, gentle and simple, poets and statesmen, soldiers, sailors, and solid merchants, once held in honour upon 'Change,[6] young girls, wives, husbands, mothers, fathers, and representatives of every age and class of man, take their repose under the dingy grass. Their very multitude surely must give them some protection, and a sense of fellowship . . . for they all died in the same faith, with common speech and aspiration, in their own fatherland.

Under the poplar-tree, its leaves just falling, golden in the autumn frost, there lies a wilding. No one is near with whom in the long nights of rain and winter he can exchange a word.

The prosperous citizens, in their well-cared-for tombs, with their trim beds above them often gay with flowers, even in death appear to look askance at the new Christian, with his wolf above the cross. No one to place even a bunch of violets on his grave, although the pious hand that buried him, perhaps in foresight of the loneliness certain to overtake the Long Wolf, lost in the thick ranks of palefaces, has placed in two glass cases (one of them is cracked) some artificial pansies — perhaps for thought, perhaps for recollection — all is one, for thought and recollection fade into one another almost insensibly.

On what forgotten creek, in what lost corner of the Dakotas, where once his race lorded it over buffalo and mustang, the Long Wolf first saw light, I have as little knowledge as of the composition of the mysterious thing that gave him life, accompanied him throughout his days, and then departed into the nothingness from whence it came.

I see the teepees set by the river's side, with the thin smoke that rises from the Indians' parsimonious fire curling out through the poles. The wolfish-looking dogs lie sleeping at the lee side of them; children play in the sun the strange and quiet games that Indian children play. Out on the prairie feed the horses under guard. Amongst these quiet children Long Wolf must have played, lassoed the dogs, or shot his little arrows at the birds. From his youth upward he must have been a rider patient and painstaking as the Indians are with horses, without the dash and fire that characterise the Western men and Mexicans.

At seventeen or eighteen, when he had assumed the name that now so strangely differentiates him from all those with whom he lies, he must have taken part in many a war-party. Upon the trail, strung out in a long line, he must have ridden with the other braves, silent and watchful, holding the horse-hair bridle with the high, light touch that every Indian has by nature and so few Europeans can acquire. He must have suffered hunger, thirst, fatigue, and all the dangers incidental to the life of those days on the plains long ere the railroad crossed them and when the buffalo migrated annually, in countless thousands, followed by the attendant packs of wolves. What his adventures were, how many scalps he took, and what atrocities he saw committed, only he himself could tell, and Indians keep no diaries except in memory.

Little by little, as the West was day by day invaded by the whites, the buffalo grew scarcer and game was difficult to kill, he and the tribe would find their means of livelihood filched from them and their position insecure. Whether the chief took part in the great fight upon the Little Bighorn,[7] or later joined the Ghost Dancers in their pathetic struggle,[8] is a sealed book to all but him who brought the Long Wolf over in his company, and he has joined the chief on the last trail.

It is best perhaps we should know nothing, for, after all, what most concerns those who pass by his grave, rendered more lonely than if it had been dug out on the prairie, by the crowd of monuments of alien folk who crowd about it, is that he lies there, waiting for the last war-whoop, uncared-for and alone.

Whether his children, if he had any, talk of his death in the strange city, buried in fog and gloom, so vast and noisy, with its life so circumscribed by customs and by laws, remains a problem never to be solved. How and of what disease he died is long forgotten by the men who pass his tombstone so unheedingly. His spirit may have returned to the region of the Red Pipestone Quarry, or ride in some wild heaven, where buffalo are ever plentiful, grass green, and water ever running, that the Creator of the Indians must have prepared for them, as he is all-wise and merciful.

It may be that it still haunts hovering above the grave under the poplar-tree. I like to think, when all is hushed in the fine summer nights, and even London sleeps, that the wolf carved on the tomb takes life upon itself, and in the air resounds the melancholy wild cry from which the sleeper took his name.

'Twould be mere justice; but as justice is so scarce on earth, that it may well be rare even in heaven, 'twere better ears attuned to the light footfall of the unshod cayuse and the soft swishing of the lodge-poles through the grass behind the travois-pony should never open.

The long-drawn cry would only break the sleeper's rest, and wake him to a world unknown and unfamiliar, where he would find no friends except the sculptured wolf.

Let him sleep on.

NOTES

1. From *Redeemed* (London: Heinemann, 1927). First published in *Scribner's Magazine* (New York), 69 (June 1921), 651-54.
2. London: Duckworth, 1902. Graham and Hudson were close friends and kindred spirits, as their letters, especially on matters of the pampa, indicate. See W. H. Hudson's *Letters to R. B. Cunninghame Graham*, edited by Richard Curle (London: Golden Cockerel Press, 1941).
3. It should, of course be Captain Jack of the Modocs, as the Indian chief Kintpuash (1837?-73) was known. After escaping from the Klamath reservation where he and his people were confined, he fought against the whites in the Modoc War 1872-73 before being captured and hanged.
4. "I too am a painter."
5. Graham is referring here to his 1914-18 War mission in Latin America buying horses for the British government to be used at the front in Europe.
6. The place where merchants meet for business transactions. Since 1800 the form has been 'Change i.e. Exchange.
7. Little Bighorn River in Wyoming and Montana. U.S. soldiers under General George A. Custer were wiped out (25 June 1876) by Indians, especially the Sioux, under Crazy Horse and Sitting Bull.
8. See the first of the "Three Letters on the Indian Question" entitled "The American Indians," subtitled "Ghosts Dancing."

EDITOR'S PREFACE

This sketch is about an incident in New Orleans, an important place for Graham and his wife, since it represents their first (1879) and last (1881) contact with the New World. In fact his first letter home from North America was from New Orleans and represents his initial impressions of that city, where he was to stay but a couple of weeks before moving on, as he had planned, to Texas. Before the young couple left finally for Europe in the spring of 1881, it appears that Gabrielle had already moved back to New Orleans when Robert was off horse-hunting in the South West and investigating ranching possibilities in Argentina. Gabrielle obviously felt much more comfortable in the comparatively civilised French city of New Orleans than she did in the dangerous border country of Texas, surrounded by marauding Indians, crude Texans, and thieving Mexicans, if we are to believe the letters. Besides, with her native command of the French language and her ability to teach painting, New Orleans was a more suitable place for her talents than the wild west.

Once again chronologically and geographically, the circularity is apt. Artistically "A Hundred in the Shade" corresponds also, since, being one of Graham's later sketches, it reflects something of his stylistic evolution and philosophical maturation. Two aspects of the story are striking: the theme of the elegant, tender-hearted prostitute, which one finds in other Graham stories e.g. "Un Monsieur" (*Hope*) and "Un Autre Monsieur" (*Charity*); and the technique that he uses to tell his story i.e. the group of men gathered on this occasion on a boat (it can be round a camp fire, on the range, in a drawing room), giving the narrator an opportunity to tell his story of unrequited love.

Departing from New Orleans in 1881 Graham was never to return to North America. In this sense "A Hundred in the Shade" was his North American swan song, the last sketch to be inspired by his two year stay on this continent.

A HUNDRED IN THE SHADE[1]

The river looked like a stream of oil flowing between the walls of dense, impenetrable woods that fringed its banks. Now and again it eddied strongly and seemed to boil, as some great rock or snag peeped up menacingly. Then it flowed on again resistlessly, bearing upon its yellow flood great trunks of bongos or of ceibas, as if they were but reeds. Toucans, looking as if they had been fashioned rather by Gian Baptista Porta[2] than by nature, darted like kingfishers across its face. Parrots screeched harshly, and above the tallest trees, macaws, blue, red and orange, soared like hawks, looking as fitting to their natural surroundings as rooks in England cawing in the elms. Upon the sandbanks great saurians basked, and when they felt the passing steamer's wash, rolled into the stream, as noiselessly as water-rats in a canal.

Now and again a little clearing broke the hostile wall of the fierce-growing vegetation, with a few straw-thatched huts, a mango tree or two, and a small patch of maize or yucca, with an unsubstantial fence of canes. Occasionally, where a stretch of plain intervened between the woods, a lean vaquero on a leaner horse, his hat blown back, forming a sort of aureole of straw behind his head, galloped along the banks after a point of steers, or merely raced the steamer for a few hundred yards and then, checking his horse, wheeled like a bird upon the wing. The steamer, painted a dazzling white, with decks piled one upon another till it looked like a floating house, belched out its thin wood smoke and panted as it fought the powerful, almost invisible current of the oily stream. Upon each side a barge was lashed, carrying a load of cattle that diminished day by day, as one was slaughtered every morning, in full sight of its doomed fellows, whose hooves were dyed red with the blood that flowed upon the deck.

As the boat forced its way upstream the heat grew daily greater, and the fierce glare from the surface of the water more intense. The sun set in a dull, red orb, and from the banks there rose a thin, white mist. From the recesses of the forests came the cries of wild animals, silent by day, but roused into activity at night. The monkeys howled their full-throated chorus, jaguars and wild cats snarled, and in the stillness the brushwood rustled as some nocturnal animal passed through them stealthily. Clouds of mosquitoes filled the air, rendering sleep impossible. Even the freshness of the evening seemed to wear away as night wore on, and one by one the jaded passengers sought the topmost deck-house to try to catch the breeze.

Sprawling in wicker chairs, as the steamer forged along, the great black banks of vegetation sliding towards her as she passed, the passengers, mopping themselves and killing the mosquitoes now and then with a loud slap, relapsed into a moody silence, as they sipped iced drinks. Now and then someone cursed the heat, and now and then one or another of the perspiring band would walk to the thermometer, hung between the windows of the deck-house, and then exclaim, "Jesus! a hundred in the shade." One of the group of men who looked at him as a ship-wrecked sailor might look out for a sail, said, "In the moon, you mean," and sank back on his chair with as much elasticity as a sponge thrown out of a bath rebounds upon the floor.

At last, rounding a bend, a light breeze ruffled the surface of the river and brought a little life into the men lounging in their deck-chairs. No one could think of sleep in such conditions. Talk languished after a few general remarks about the price of cattle, and the usual stories about the prowess of the horses, the best in the whole world, that everyone had owned, for general conversation usually flags in a society of men, when women and horses have been discussed. No one spoke for a considerable time, as the steamer swept along through the dark alley of the woods, illuminated by a thousand million fire-flies flashing among the trees. The dark, blue southern sky, and the yellow waters of the stream, lighted up by the powerful port and starboard lights, appeared to frame the vessel in, and cut her off from all the world.

Without preamble, the orchid hunter, a thin, sunburned man, spectacled and bald, took up his parable.[3] He told of having camped alone in Singapore, and being bitten on the forefinger of his left hand by some poisonous snake or other. "I had no antidote of any kind with me. My whisky bottle was quite empty. Not that I think it would have done much good had it been full, for I was so well soaked in it, I should have been obliged to drink a quart before it took effect on me. Yes, well, we orchid hunters as a rule are not teetotallers. Perhaps the damp, the solitude, or God knows what, soon drives most of us to drink. What did I do? Oh, yes, I sawed the finger off with a jack-knife. Of course it hurt; but it was just root hog or die. The worst of it is that the mosquitoes always fasten on the stump." He held up a brown mutilated hand for us to look at and then, after a long pull at his iced drink, sank back again into the silence that had become a second nature to him. Perhaps to those who practise orchid hunting it seems indecent to be talking in the primeval silence of the woods.

To the disjointed story of the orchid hunter, that seemed to be extracted from him almost against his will, succeeded the impresario of a travelling operetta company, fluent and full of New York slang and jokes designed to please the intelligence of infant cavemen, long before wit or humour humanised the world. Withal not a bad fellow, for a man whose company, by his own confession, was half a brothel, and as difficult to drive as a whole waggon load of apes. A ranch man brought a whiff of purer air into the symposium, and as he sat tapping his leg with an imaginary whip, his thumb turned upwards from constant using of the lasso, his soft and soothing Western voice acted as a soporific on the company. They listened half awake to a long tale about the prowess of a Flathead Indian horse, "a buck-skin and a single footer, why, that yer hoice would pick a animal out of a bunch of steers, he knowed a fat one, too, better than a human, sure he did, that little hoice."

To him succeeded a traveller in a patent medicine that would cure snakebites, shingles, coughs, colds, and rheumatism. "What about earthquakes?" ejaculated someone. "Well, my stuff doesn't lay out to stop 'em; but it does no harm to 'em, anyway, and maybe might do some good to the survivors if they took it soon enough." He told us that he had never taken it himself, preferring good, sound whisky, but added, "I am its prophet, anyhow. 'One God, one Zamolina,'⁴ as good a creed as any other as far as I can see, and one a man can hold without much danger to his conscience, as long as the stuff sells."

The laugh that greeted the exposition of the creed of the patent medicine philosopher died away, and it appeared the experiences of the company had been exhausted. Confession, no matter if auricular or *coram publico*, generally extorts confession. Seated in the shade, so that up to the moment of his speaking no one had observed him, there was a quiet man, dressed in immaculate white clothes. His hundred dollar jipijapa hat lay beside him on the deck. Somewhere about fifty years of age, his thick, dark hair was just beginning to turn grey. Tall and athletic-looking, he still had not the look of being used to frontier life, and his quiet voice and manner showed him to have received what for the want of any better word is styled education, a thing that, though it can do nothing to improve the faculties, yet now and then gives them the power of self-expression, in natures previously dumb.

"I don't know why I should tell you or anybody," he said, "this tale, experience or what you like to call it, except that as it happened to me twenty years ago today, it seems impersonal and as if it had occurred to some one I had known. I was young then." He paused and drew himself up a little, as a well-preserved man of fifty does when he refers to himself as old, all the time feeling women still turn round to look at him as he passes on the street. "I was young then. . . . It was in New Orleans that I met her, an English girl, living alone, *faisant la cocotte*.⁵ as they say down there. I think it was in the St. Charles Hotel that I first saw her. Tall and red-haired, not too fat, not too thin, as the Arabs say when speaking of a handsome woman. What her real name was I never knew. I liked her far too well ever to wish to pry into her life. Her *nom de guerre* was Daphne Villiers, and by that name I knew and by degrees began to love her. She lived in one of those old streets that run into Lafayette Square, in the French quarter of the town. I forgot to say she spoke all languages, French, Spanish and Italian, German, and God knows what, indifferently well. A rare thing for an Englishwoman, even of her profession.

"Her rooms were furnished, not in the style you might expect, big looking-glasses, Louis Quinze chairs and tables, with reproductions of the Bath of Psyche, Venus and Cupid, French prints of women bathing, as 'Les Biches à la Mer', or 'La Puce', showing a girl of ample charms catching a flea upon her leg, but simply and in good taste. Two or three bits of china, good but inexpensive, with one fine piece of Ming, and a Rhodes plate or two were dotted here and there. Upon the walls were a few engravings of French pictures, with one or two water-colours and a pastel of herself, done, as she said, in Paris by a well-known pastelist, with the signature carefully erased. What struck me most about the rooms was a small cabinet of books. Anatole France and Guy de Maupassant,[6] some poetry, with Adah Mencken's verses,[7] and some manuals on china and on furniture, with *Manon Lescaut*,[8] Dante's *Vita Nouva*[9] and the *Heptameron*[10] are what I recollect.

"There was a piano that she said 'of course is necessary in the métier,' on which she played not very well and sang French Creole songs with rather a good voice. Not having much to do at that time, I got to dropping in upon her whenever she was not engaged, not so much as a lover, but to enjoy a talk with someone whose mind did not entirely run upon the price of cotton, the sale of real estate, railway shares, dividends, the things in fact that citizens of 'God's own country' chiefly converse about to the exclusion of all else. Curiously enough, I was never jealous, although she often had to postpone my visits on account of her work. Of course, after the fashion of most women of her class, she always talked about 'my work'. She said she never drank except when she was working and I rather think that the use of the word kept me from being jealous, for I flattered myself she never used it when speaking of my visits to her.

"Little by little we grew almost indispensable to one another. I lent her books and literary magazines. How well I recollect bringing her *L'Imitation de Jésus*[11] and how she laughed, saying she knew it all by heart. 'Twas only then I found out that she was a Catholic; not that she cared too much for her religion, but as she said, the Mass with all there is about it, lights, incense and the tradition of antiquity, appealed to her on the aesthetic side. Yes, well, yes, I got to love her, and to look forward to our long talks on books and china, pictures and the like. I never took her out to theatres, for she said people would think that she was 'working' if they saw me with her, and she looked upon me as a friend. I liked to hear her say so, for as time went on we had become quite as much friends as lovers, and I used to tell her everything that had happened to me since my last visit to her.

"She on her part used to advise me, as all women will advise the man they love. Though their advice may not be very weighty, yet a man is a fool who does not profit by it. One evening I went to see her, taking a big bunch of flowers, and when she thanked me I said, 'Congratulate me too, this is my birthday.' To my surprise she burst out crying, and for a long time I could not make her tell me the reason of her tears. At last she said, 'I should have liked to give you something, but you know how I live and I am sure you will not take a present from me.' Nothing that I could say would pacify her, although I swore that I would value anything she gave. For a long time she sobbed convulsively, till at last, drying her tears up with a handkerchief, she smiled and coming up to me, threw her arms round my neck and said, 'I have one thing that I can give you, that belongs entirely to me, that is myself.'

"Business kept me from seeing her again for several days. The more I thought about her, the more certain it appeared I could not live without her. So on the first opportunity I sought the curious old winding street in the French quarter of the town. The house looked strangely silent, and after knocking at the door for a long time the coloured girl I knew so well opened it, crying, holding a letter and a little packet in her hand. 'Missy Daphne, she done gone away,' she said, and looked at me reproachfully, as I thought afterwards. The letter told me she had gone off to Tampico with a mining engineer, not a bad fellow, who she thought would marry her. She said she had acted for the best, for both of us, and asked me to accept the little piece of Chinese pottery I so often had admired."

The story-teller ceased his tale just as a bird stops singing, when you expect he will go on. Silence fell on the hearers. It may be some of them had had presents on their birthdays, of less value than the teller's of the tale. No one said anything except the ranch man with the directness of a simple soul: "Reckon you missed the round-up that time, friend." The story-teller nodded at him, and walking up to the thermometer, muttered, "A hundred in the shade."

NOTES

1. From *Redeemed* (London: Heinemann, 1927). First published in *Saturday Review*, 140 (5 May 1925), 652-55.

2. This is probably, rather, Giovanni da Udine (Giovanni Nanni) (1487-64), Italian painter, decorative artist and architect, a pupil of Raphael, whose early interest in animals influenced his artistic career. His decorative work in stucco and fresco was imitated in England by eighteenth-century neoclassical designers. Graham would probably also know his occasional tendency to indulge in grotesque ornamentation.

3. cf. Graham's sketch "Animula Vagula" (also from *Redeemed*), renamed "The Orchid Hunter" by Tschiffely in his anthology *Rodeo* (London: Heinemann, 1936).

4. This obscure reference might be a Graham variation of Zamorin, or Zamorine, a Hindu sovereign or emperor. Given the Spanish tradition of the Golden Age, the union of the altar and the throne, and the theory of the Divine Right of Kings, the notion of "One God, One Emperor" is an acceptable, or at least a possible, interpretation of this saying.

5. Living as a prostitute.

6. Anatole France (1844-1924), French writer of philosophical and satirical fiction that is often anti-religious e.g. *Vie de Jeanne d'Arc* (1908) and *La Révolte des Anges* (1914); and Guy de Maupassant (1850-93), French master of the realistic short story e.g. *Une Vie* (1883) and *Bel Ami* (1885).

7. Adah Isaacs Menken (1835-68), American actress and poet, whose rich garish, romantic poetry, collected as *Infelicia* (1868) was highly autobiographical.

8. From *Mémoires d'un homme de qualité* (1728-32) by l'abbé Antoine-François

Prévost (1697-1763). *L'Histoire du Chevalier Des Grieux et de Manon* is the sentimental love story of a weak passionate young man and a girl intended for the convent, who elope to Louisiana where Manon dies of exhaustion.

9. *La vita nuova* (1292) of the Italian master Dante Alighieri (1265-1321) tells of his youthful devotion to Beatrice.

10. Collection of tales of love composed by Marguerite, sister of Francis I, Queen of Navarre (1492-1549). Originally called *Contes de la Reine de Navarre*, the *Heptameron* title (meaning seven days, cf. *Decameron*) was given by a later editor.

11. *The Imitation of Christ* by Thomas à Kempis (*c.* 1380-1471), German theologian of the Low Countries. *L'Imitation de Jésus-Christ* (1662), is the best known and still current translation by Le Maître de Saci, Louis-Isaac (1613-84), of this famous devotional work of prayer.

EDITOR'S PREFACE

I have chosen to close this collection with Don Roberto's version of part of Tschiffely's famous ride from Buenos Aires to New York. I think it is doubly appropriate since (i) part of Tschiffely's trek was a re-run of the return journey made by Robert and Gabriela from Mexico to Texas in 1880 before Tschiffely even knew Graham. In fact, Tschiffely published his own book-length description of the trip the year after Graham's sketch — *Tschiffely's Ride* (London: Heinemann, 1933); and (ii) Tschiffely was to become Graham's biographer just a few years later. But at the time of writing this sketch Graham had not even met Tschiffely. With the coming together of their lives, and Graham's sharing his letters, stories, memories (and a few fictions?) with the young writer, this shadowy North American part of Graham's life was to be made public. As we have noted, the 1937 biography, rather than clarifying many aspects of Graham's Texas visit, simply added to the confusion. But whatever criticism we might have of Tschiffely's work today, for several decades it was an important source of information for scholars. Besides, his intentions were always good.

I have edited this sketch to include only the parts of Tschiffely's celebrated ride that correspond to the area under discussion in this volume i.e. Mexico, Texas and South West U.S.A. Thus, descriptions of the author's experiences from Argentina, through Bolivia, Ecuador, Colombia, Panama, Costa Rica, El Salvador and Guatemala, before finally reaching Mexico, although fascinating, have been omitted from this particular collection. Little did Graham know when he compiled this narrative of Tschiffely's ride from Argentine newspapers (especially *La Nación*), that the young Swiss-Argentine horseman would return the favour, and record for posterity Graham's own earlier travels in the same region. In a sense I am repaying both masters by anthologising "Tschiffely's Ride" as seen through the eyes of Don Roberto. No other ending could be more fitting — unless, of course, I were to make the same journey and give *my* impressions of the same trip, keeping in mind Tschiffely's version of Graham's trek, or Graham's rendering of Tschiffely's epic ride, or . . . The possibilities of the magic number three, as of all art, are infinite.

TSCHIFFELY'S RIDE[1]

Tschiffely,[2] Mancha and Gato.[3] The three names are as indivisible as the three Persons of the Trinity.

They will go down to history in the Argentine with far more certainty than those of many worthy politicians, gold-laced generals, diplomats, and others who have strutted their brief hour upon the stage of the republic.

Tschiffely in his various letters to the press during his three years' journey from Buenos Aires to New York, reveals his sympathetic personality.

Writing from Washington, on April 26th, 1928, to *La Asociación Militar de Retirados del Ejército y Armada*, Buenos Aires, he signs, "Tschiffely, Mancha y Gato." On other occasions he says, "remembrances and neighs, from the horses."

Tschiffely, a Swiss long settled in the Argentine, a famous horseman, is a man of iron resolution and infinite resource, as his great feat, perhaps the greatest that man and horses have performed in all the history of the world, is there to show.

As to the horses, their deeds speak better for them than any words . . .

How, when or wherefore it came into Tschiffely's head to announce his raid from Buenos Aires to New York is to me as unknown as most of the designs of fate.

Immediately the local Babbitry gave tongue. Old babblers and young bletherers rushed into print to show it was impossible. Just as in Salamanca, when the wise reverend fools proved mathematically and theologically that Columbus was a madman, so did the local wiseacres demonstrate Tschiffely was an ass. No horses, so they said, bred in the plains, almost at sea-level, could cross the Andes, still less endure the tropics, or bear the constant change of climate and of food upon the road. Indians and bandits would attack the rider; wild beasts destroy the horses; their feet would give out on the stony mountain roads. In fact the project was absurd and would bring ridicule upon the country. Tschiffely took no notice of the arm-chair riders and quietly went on with his few preparations for the start. They were soon made, and he proceeded to the south, where the most hardy animals are bred, to choose the horses that became national heroes. He selected two, Mancha, a skewbald, with white legs and face, and streaked all over with white stripes, stocky and with well-made legs and feet, like those of a male mule, as hard as steel. His second choice was Gato, a yellow dun, for *gato* is a contraction of the word *gateado* (literally, cat-coloured), the favourite colour of the gauchos of the plains, who always used to choose that colour for hard work. They have a saying, "Gateado, antes muerto que cansado," a dun horse dies before he tires.

Azara, the Spanish naturalist, writing in 1785 (?)[4], says that the great troops of wild horses, known as *baguales*, that in his time roamed all over the pampas, from San Luis to Patagonia, were nearly all either some shade of dun or brown. Mancha was fifteen years of age, and Gato fourteen, and neither of them had ever eaten corn or worn a shoe.

The horses had just finished a journey of nine hundred miles, taking a troop of cattle from Sarmiento, far below the Welsh settlement of Chubut,[5] to Ayacucho in the province of Buenos Aires, in the month of March.

One road and only one was open to him, across the plains to Mendoza, then over the Andes and along the coast of Chile and Peru, from Ecuador to Colombia and through Panama to Nicaragua and on to Mexico.

Once there, Tschiffely knew, all would be easy and the victory assured, for Mexico presented no essential difficulty with its great open plains, and with a population that adored the horse, almost as much as do the Argentines.

Tschiffely set out from Buenos Aires in April, 1925, riding his Mancha and leading Gato with a pack-saddle carrying his food and clothes . . .

When he arrived at San José de Costa Rica in a torrential rain after a forced march of eight leagues, a deputation waited on him with an invitation to a banquet. He was wet to the skin, his boots were sandals tied to his feet with strips of hide. After he had seen Mancha and Gato led off in honour, guests of the Legation of the Argentine, his head whirling with the champagne that he was forced to drink, he staggered to his room in the hotel. A bed with sheets, the first he had seen for months, was so inviting that, wet through as he was, without attempting even to remove his fragmentary boots, he threw himself upon it, and fell asleep. He says he was exhausted, but that the horses were as fresh as when they had started out from Panama.

His health obliged him to remain for several weeks in Panama. As Nicaragua was in a state bordering on anarchy, a prey to the contending factions, swarming with bandits and disbanded soldiers, and horses were extremely scarce, and, of course, contraband of war, he was obliged once more to embark his horses a little distance from Puntarenas (Costa Rica) to La Unión in Salvador.

The journey through that small republic was not difficult, but the heat was so intense that it brought out a new attack of the malaria, and in San Salvador (the capital of the republic of El Salvador) he was laid up another fifteen days. His strength exhausted by the hardships of the road and the attacks of fever that he suffered from, he doubted for the first time since he left Buenos Aires of his ultimate success.

However, when he reached Guatemala City, at an altitude of six thousand feet, he soon revived in spirits and in health.

"We" were warmly welcomed by the inhabitants and the Government; society and the learned institutions all joined in honouring "us". The phrase shows the man's character, as well as a whole volume of his "life and miracles." Mancha and Gato, without doubt, were flattered by the attention of the "cultured institutions," and if they could have spoken would probably have done as well as or better than many orators such institutions endure and suffer under.

Tschiffely now felt certain of success. Mexico was a land where gentlemen and horsemen (*caballero*) were synonymous. The country on the whole was not so difficult as any through which he had passed. His hopes ran high, and in a week or two he thought he would be in the capital (Mexico).

But as the Spanish proverb has it, a hare springs up when you are not expecting her ("Adonde menos se piensa, salta la liebre").

Not far from the bridge at the frontier Gato went lame for the first time since leaving Buenos Aires. At Tapachula he could go no farther. Luckily there was a military post of cavalry. The veterinary surgeon found that the smith in Guatemala had driven a nail into the foot. He cut it out at once, but the hot climate and the perpetual moisture of the rainy season inflamed the wound so much that Tschiffely passed three or four nights, so to speak, at the bedside of the sufferer, applying fomentations to the foot. Gato was almost well, when some "son of a mother who never yet said no" let loose overnight a strange horse in the stable-yard. Next morning Gato had received so terrible a kick on his near foreleg that he could not lie down. The leg swelled up enormously and everyone told Tschiffely that the best thing that he could do was to shoot Gato and end his misery.

"It was a rude blow and I was overwhelmed with grief, but I would not even entertain the idea of losing the good horse, companion of 'our' perils on the road."

At once he telegraphed to the Argentine Ambassador in the capital, Señor Roberto Labougli, who replied asking him to send the horse by train to Mexico, where he would be cared for by the best veterinaries.

These delays made him lose a month, but nothing daunted, having procured a guide and bought two horses for him, he once more started out upon the road.

Three or four days' journey convinced him that he would never reach the capital alone, for the road swarmed with bandits and with revolutionaries, words that, as he says, in Mexico have the same meaning.

At the next military post the commandant refused to let him pass, saying he could not respond for his security if he went on alone.

Hearing the case, the President of the Republic, General Elías Calles, sent out a troop of cavalry to escort Tschiffely on the road.

This was a "gesture," as he says, of 'the greatest generosity and sympathy to the Argentine Republic never before accorded to a mere traveller." The truth was that Mexico was all agog to see the "heroes" of the raid.

At every town and hamlet that he passed the inhabitants turned out to greet him, patting and making much of Mancha and doing all that lay within their power to help them on their way.

Even in the humble ranchos of the Indians "they did their best to succour and assist us."

The rains delayed the journey, and the cavalry were not well mounted, so that when they reached Oscara, Mancha alone was not exhausted.

The rivers, too, were swollen with the rains and, as there were no bridges, had to be crossed swimming — a dangerous operation, as they swarmed with alligators. As he advanced amidst general rejoicing, encountering a cooler climate day by day, for the interior plateau of the country ("la meseta de Anáhuac") stands at an elevation of six thousand feet, the road grew easier.

At Puebla, the people had arranged a festival "to welcome us," but as fate willed it, he had at once to take to bed, for several days prostrated by malaria.

When he reached Mexico his entry was a triumph, and was telegraphed at once to the whole world.

The streets were packed and as he rode along on Mancha, women came out upon the balconies and showered flowers upon him.

"My joy was without limit, and my feelings unforgettable, when I saw 'friend Gato' ('el amigo Gato') led up quite fresh, and as sound as when he was a colt," owing to the care he had received from the State veterinary, Señor Labougle.[6] During his sojourn in the city he received enormous hospitality from all classes of society, the President himself visiting the horses several times and admiring them.

On the 27th of November he set his face towards the frontier of the United States, leaving a host of friends in Mexico, with both his horses fresh and bounding under him. All through Mexico Tschiffely's journey was a triumphal march, for the news of his coming had been telegraphed from Mexico to every town upon the way. His stages were erratic, for at times more than a hundred horsemen turned out to escort him on his way. The smallest hamlet hoisted the Argentine flag, sometimes made out of coloured paper, and the nine hundred miles to New Laredo, the frontier town upon the Río Grande, was like a street during a carnival, that is to say, when they passed through a town. I, who have ridden the whole distance from San Antonio, Texas, to Mexico, and back again, when all the road was perilous from the attacks of the Apaches near the frontier, and of the bandits, nearer Mexico, though I remember every village he passed through, can hardly take in the changed circumstances. Across the frontier the authorities had organised a military pageant in honour "of the brave horseman of the Argentine and his two faithful friends." Tschiffely, mounted on Mancha and holding Gato by his side, took the salute, as the troops with their bands playing passed before him. It must have been the proudest moment of his life, and [must] have repaid him for all that he had undergone on his fantastic journey of fifteen thousand miles.

Two thousand kilometres still lay between the frontier and his goal, and perils of a sort he had not looked for still awaited him. He had hoped to reach New York in June, but invitations, banquets and interviews rained on him. If he had not protested, escorts of cavalry would have accompanied him all through Texas. In San Antonio he was obliged to stay for fifteen days, the guest of the municipality. The same thing happened in Austin, Houston, Fort Worth and Dallas, and invitations from towns far off his route flowed in upon him. When in Fort Worth, a compatriot, Don Gustavo Muñiz Barreto, fitted him out with a complete gaucho costume, poncho, and wide Turkish trousers, tucked into high patent-leather boots, with silver trappings for his horse. Public enthusiasm knew no bounds. Mancha, on account of his striking colour, was the idol of "las bellas Yanquis," who flocked to see him every day, patting and petting him. They grew so demonstrative in their affection that Tschiffely had to keep strict guard over Mancha or they would have cut off all his mane and tail to keep as souvenirs.

Mancha, who, as we know, enjoyed "fame as a buckjumper," became so irritable that it was dangerous to go near him; but Gato, more apathetic, took everything "con apatía," and was concerned entirely with the good things of the stable, which he consumed with great enthusiasm.

Both of them grew as fat as Jeshurun,[7] but there is no recorded instance of their ever having kicked.

Once more the local wiseacres shook their long ears and solemnly announced that no horse in the world could stand more than a day or two upon the treated roads. In spite of that, Mancha and Gato advanced steadily, doing their thirty miles a day, passing by St. Louis, Missouri, Indianapolis, and Washington.

As they drew nearer to New York the danger that they ran from the continuous stream of automobiles on the roads was as great as on any portion of his adventurous road. As he rode on, in constant peril from the motor traffic, his mind dwelt always on his goal, and on the joy that he would feel when once again he and his horses arrived safely in Buenos Aires, where, after all their perils and hard work, Gato and Mancha could forget for ever girths, bits and saddles, and the hardships of the road. His dream is fulfilled, and the two faithful companions of his wanderings once more are back again in their own country, after having travelled fifteen thousand miles during their three years' raid. Happier than mankind, they have their Trapalanda upon earth, eat the sweet grasses of their native plains, drink the soft, muddy water of some *arroyo*, and though they know it not, never again "the cruel spur shall make them weary."

NOTES

1. From *Writ in Sand* (London: Heinemann, 1932).
2. "I did not know Tschiffely when I wrote this sketch, taking my information from Argentine papers and magazines" (Graham's footnote).
   Aimé F. Tschiffely (1895-1954), Swiss-Argentine horseman and writer who, apart from his famous ride and his biography of Don Roberto, is the author of *Bridle Paths* (1936), *This Way Southward*

(1945), *Corichancha* (1943), *Bohemia Junction* (1950), *Round and About Spain* (1952), plus other adventure and travel books.

3. Immortalised in Tschiffely's *The Tale of Two Horses* (1934). When Graham made his farewell journey to Argentina in 1936, he took two bags of oats for Tschiffely's faithful horses. On Don Roberto's death in Buenos Aires on 20 March 1936, Mancha and Gato walked behind his hearse, led by two gauchos.

4. Felix de Azara, *Apuntamientos para la historia natural de los cuadrúpedos del Paraguay y Río de la Plata*. 2 vols. (Madrid, 1802). Graham's questioning of the date is justified.

5. See for example, Bernabé Martínez Ruiz, *La colonización galesa en el valle del Chubut* (Buenos Aires: Editorial Galerna, 1977); Geraint D. Owen, *Crisis in Chubut* (Swansea: Christopher Davies, 1977); Glyn Williams, *The Desert and the Dream* (Cardiff: University of Wales Press, 1975).

6. I think that it is too much of a coincidence that the Mexican veterinary surgeon mentioned here, and the Argentine Ambassador mentioned just previously (p. 134), should have such similar but unusual names — Labougle/Labougli. This seems like a case of Graham's having confused his notes taken from the original Argentine newspaper sources.

7. An affectionate, poetical name for Israel found in the Old Testament.

GLOSSARY

This glossary is designed solely to help the reader appreciate more the foregoing sketches. It is not meant to be specialist, technical or exhaustive, nor does it try to provide all the alternative meanings of the words and phrases listed. Its express function is related only to the sketches contained in this volume.

abarrotes groceries

aguacate avocado pear

agujereado(a) full of holes, perforated

ahuehuete Mexican cypress

alameda tree-lined public walk or promenade

alcalde mayor, magistrate

alhóndiga open-air market surrounded by covered porticoes

alkali grass that grows in alkaline soil

aloe succulent plant

Arapaho(e) Algonquin people ranging over the plains region from southern Saskatchewan and Manitoba to New Mexico and Texas

arroba weight (25 pounds)

arroyo stream

atole corn meal cooked and eaten as mush or drunk like gruel

bagual wild horse (without master)

bando edict, proclamation

barajo! Dammit! Hell! (variation of **carajo!**)

bayou creek, stream

biche hind, doe; darling

bolsón flat-floored desert valley

bongo tropical American timber tree

bucephalus riding horse, usually spirited

caballada team of horses

calumet ceremonial peace pipe of the Indians

capataz foreman

carajo! Dammit! Hell!

cayuse Indian pony

ceiba large tropical American tree

cerro hill

cinch strong girth for a pack or saddle

claco, tlaco small copper coin used in nineteenth-century Mexico

coram publico in public

corregidor Spanish magistrate in Latin America

côtelettes à la milanaise chops done Milanese style

Coyotero Indians of an Apache division

Creole French patois spoken in Louisiana region

crucecita little cross

cuarta whip

cuesta slope, hill

cura parish priest

chaparral dense thicket of shrubs or trees

chaparreras, chaps leather leggings

charco pool of stagnant water

cherimoya, chirimoya fruit like the custard apple

défroque(s) cast-off clothing

diapason tuning fork

Digger member of a short-lived egalitarian group in seventeenth-century England that cultivated common lands as a protest

doodlebug small local train

dulcero seller of sweets

dulces sweets

empyrean heaven

enceinte enclosed area

encrucijada crossroad, intersection

fiero wild, savage
fierro iron (in plural, sometimes money)
fondak inn
frijol bean (kidney), black bean

gachupín Spanish settler in South America (disparaging)
gateado cat-coloured
gato cat
greaser offensive name for a Mexican
guarache, huarache moccasin, sandal
guisache, huisache thorny shrub or small tree (southern U.S.A.)
gules red

hegira sudden departure (cf. Mahomet's flight from persecution in Mecca.)
heliot, Heliot serf, exploited person
heller old small silver coin (Germany)
huarache, guarache moccasin, sandal
huisache, guisache thorny shrub or small tree (southern U.S.A.)

istle fibre derived from an agave plant, used for carpets, etc.

jacal crude hut with thatched roof
jarabe provincial Mexican dance
Jicarillas Apache people of the western group ranging through south-east Colorado and northern New Mexico
jipijapa hat made of fibre from jipijapa plant (like palm)

Kickapoos Indian people originally from Wisconsin, moved to Oklahoma and Chihuahua
Kiowa Tanoan people in adjoining parts of Oklahoma, Kansas, Colorado and New Mexico

lépero crook, low-class person
Lipan(e)s Apache people of eastern New Mexico and western Texas
lugs ears (Scottish)

maguey species of the aloe plant from which mescal is made
mango tropical tree
marmot rodent, like the woodchuck or groundhog

mecate horsehair, rope for tying on leading horses
medio half
mescal, mezcal Mexican liquor distilled from maguey plant
Mescalero Apache people formerly ranging through western and central Texas and eastern New Mexico
mesquite, mezquite spiny tree or shrub
mesón, meson inn
metate flat stone for grinding
mir village community common in Russia
Mohave, Mojave Indian people of Colorado River valley in Arizona, California and Nevada
monte forest, wood; also, a card game

obispo bishop
ocote torch; species of pine
Oglala, Ogalala Teton Dakota Indian people
Opata Taracahitian people of north-eastern part of Sonora, Mexico

país desconocido unknown country
pelado Mexican peon in the south west (usually disparaging)
pelón hairless Aztec dog
peña rock
Pima people of southern Arizona and New Mexico
pinole finely-ground flour made from parched corn
plátano banana
plaza de armas parade ground
poblano, poblana village (adjective), applied to girls or hats; also native of Puebla (Mexico)
puce flea (French)
pulque fermented drink made from maguey juice

quirt riding whip (especially in western U.S.A.)

rastrojo fodder
resaca undercurrent

sapote, zapote fruit of the marmalade tree

saurian reptile that resembles the lizard
schelm rogue, rascal
serape, sarape woollen blanket worn as poncho
shaddock thick-rinded, pear-shaped citrus fruit related to the grapefruit
silla saddle
sotol liquor made from maguey plant
sutler pedlar who sells goods and food to an army
Swabia duchy in medieval Germany

tamales Mexican dish made of chopped meat with crushed corn
tasajo jerked meat
tendajo village store
tequila Mexican liquor made by redistilling mescal
tessellated constructed in the style of checkered mosaic
Thuringia region in central Germany
tierra caliente hot country
tierra fría cold country

tlaco, claco small copper coin used in nineteenth-century Mexico
toquilla hatband, headscarf
tortilla flat cake made of corn meal baked on a hot sheet of iron or slab of stone
Trapalanda horse heaven of the gauchos; also, mythical city of the Indians (see W. H. Hudson's "Pelino Viera's Confession")
travois primitive vehicle hauled by horse or dog used by the Plains Indians of North America

Utes group of Shoshonean peoples of Colorado, Utah and New Mexico

vaquero cowboy

yucca liliaceous plant of southern U.S.A., Mexico and Central America

zapote, sapote fruit of the marmalade tree (and tropical fruits, in general)

BIBLIOGRAPHY

I. WORKS OF R. B. CUNNINGHAME GRAHAM

The following list of Graham's published works, excluding translations, prefaces to other writers' works, and pamphlets, contains anthologies compiled by various editors. All books, which were published in London unless otherwise indicated, are listed in chronological order of publication.

Notes on the District of Menteith. A. & C. Black, 1895.
Father Archangel of Scotland. A. & C. Black, 1896.
Mogreb-el-Acksa. Heinemann, 1898.
The Ipané. Fisher Unwin, 1899.
Thirteen Stories. Heinemann, 1900.
A Vanished Arcadia. Heinemann, 1901.
Success. Duckworth, 1902.
Hernando de Soto. Heinemann, 1903.
Progress. Duckworth, 1905.
His People. Duckworth, 1906.
Faith. Duckworth, 1909.
Hope. Duckworth, 1910.
Charity. Duckworth, 1912.
A Hatchment. Duckworth, 1913.
Scottish Stories. Duckworth, 1914.
Bernal Díaz del Castillo. Eveleigh Nash, 1915.
Brought Forward. Duckworth, 1916.
A Brazilian Mystic. Heinemann, 1920.
Cartagena and the Banks of the Sinú. Heinemann, 1922.
The Conquest of New Granada. Heinemann, 1922.
The Conquest of the River Plate. Heinemann, 1924.
Doughty Deeds. Heinemann, 1925.
Pedro de Valdivia. Heinemann, 1926.
Redeemed. Heinemann, 1927.
José Antonio Páez. Heinemann, 1929.
Thirty Tales and Sketches (selected by Edward Garnett). Heinemann, 1929.
The Horses of the Conquest. Heinemann, 1930.
Writ in Sand. Heinemann, 1932.
Portrait of a Dictator. Heinemann, 1933.
Mirages. Heinemann, 1936.

Rodeo (selected by A. F. Tschiffely). Heinemann, 1936.

The Essential R. B. Cunninghame Graham (selected by Paul Bloomfield). Cape, 1952.

Selected Short Stories (selected by Clover Pertíñez). Madrid: Alhambra, 1959.

The South American Sketches of R. B. Cunninghame Graham (selected and edited by John Walker). Norman, Oklahoma: University of Oklahoma Press, 1978.

Beattock for Moffat and the Best of R. B. Cunninghame Graham. Edinburgh: Paul Harris, 1979.

Tales of Horsemen (selected by Alexander Maitland). Edinburgh: Canongate, 1981.

Selected Writings of Cunninghame Graham (edited by Cedric T. Watts). New Jersey: Fairleigh Dickinson University Press, 1981.

The Scottish Sketches of R. B. Cunninghame Graham (selected and edited by John Walker). Edinburgh: Scottish Academic Press, 1982.

II. SELECTED STUDIES—GENERAL

West, Herbert F. *A Modern Conquistador: Robert Bontine Cunninghame Graham: His Life and Works.* Cranley and Day, 1932.

Tschiffely, Aimé F. *Don Roberto.* Heinemann, 1937.

MacDiarmid, Hugh. *Cunninghame Graham: A Centenary Study.* Glasgow: Caledonian Press, 1952.

Haymaker, Richard E. *Prince-Errant and Evocator of Horizons.* Kingsport, Tennessee: Kingsport Press, 1967.

Watts, Cedric T. and Laurence Davies. *Cunninghame Graham: A Critical Biography.* Cambridge University Press, 1979.

Watts, Cedric T. *R. B. Cunninghame Graham.* Boston: Twayne, 1983.

Maitland, Alexander. *Robert and Gabriela Cunninghame Graham.* Edinburgh: Blackwood, 1984.

III. CRITICAL STUDIES ON CUNNINGHAME GRAHAM AND THE SOUTH WEST

Apart from the appropriate sections of the general studies devoted to Mexico, Texas and the South West, the following articles are useful:

Isbell, George P. "Cunninghame Graham in Texas," *Southwestern Historical Quarterly,* XLIX, No. 4 (April 1946), 501-9.

Davies, Laurence. "'No Sense at All': Cunninghame Graham and a Texas Hanging." Unpublished article.

IV. BIBLIOGRAPHICAL WORKS ON CUNNINGHAME GRAHAM

Watts, Cedric T. "R. B. Cunninghame Graham (1852-1936): A List of his Contributions to Periodicals," *The Bibliotheck*, Vol. 4, No. 5 (1965), 186-99.

Walker, John. "A Chronological Bibliography of Works on R. B. Cunninghame Graham (1852-1936)," *The Bibliotheck*, Vol. 9, Nos. 2 and 3 (1978), 47-64.

—— "R. B. Cunninghame Graham: An Annotated Bibliography of Writings About Him," *English Literature in Transition*, Vol. 22, No. 2 (1979), 77-156.

—— *Cunninghame Graham and Scotland: An Annotated Bibliography*. Dollar: Douglas Mack, 1980.